Crocheted Mitts & Mittens

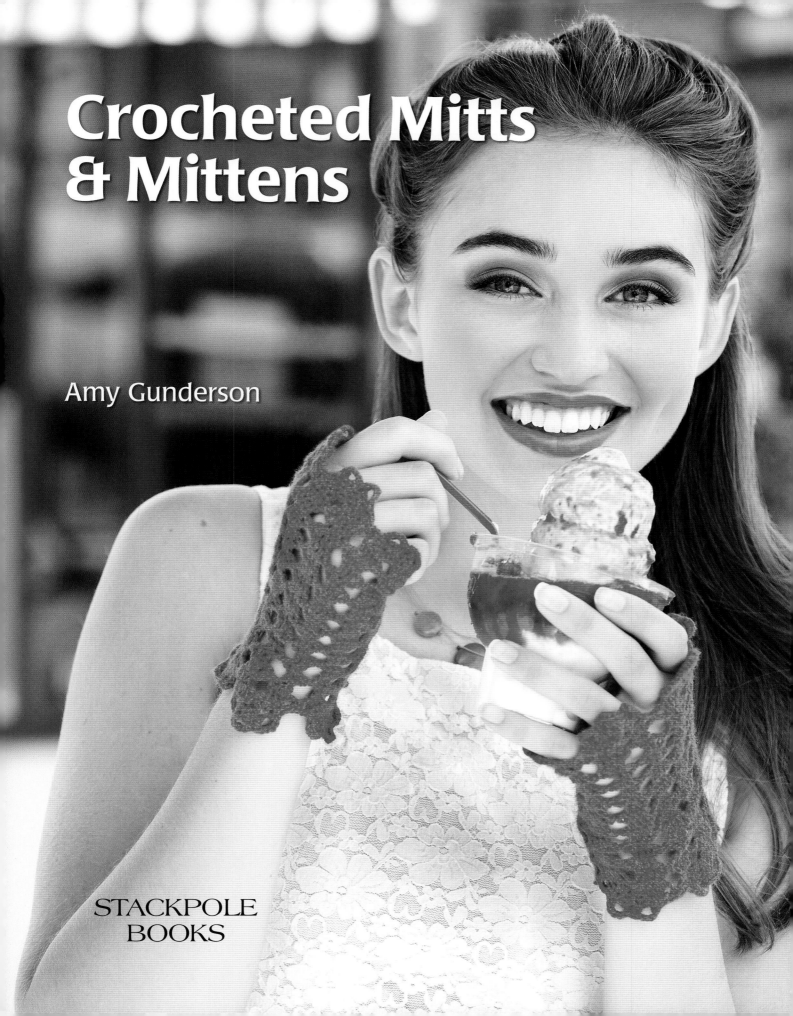

Crocheted Mitts & Mittens

Amy Gunderson

STACKPOLE
BOOKS

For Allison, I miss you.

Published by
STACKPOLE BOOKS
5067 Ritter Road
Mechanicsburg, PA 17055
www.stackpolebooks.com

Printed in the United States of America

10 9 8 7 6 5 4 3 2 1

First edition

Cover design by Wendy A. Reynolds
Project and model photography by Shane Baskin, Black Box Studios
How-to photography by Amy Gunderson

Library of Congress Cataloging-in-Publication Data

Gunderson, Amy.
  Crocheted mitts & mittens : 25 fun and fashionable designs for fingerless gloves, mittens, and wrist warmers / Amy Gunderson.
    pages cm
  ISBN 978-0-8117-1410-5
1. Crocheting—Patterns. 2. Gloves. I. Title. II. Title: Crocheted mitts and mittens.
  TT825.G78468 2015
  746.43'4—dc23
                    2014042780

Acknowledgments

A huge thanks to my friend and the photographer of the projects in this book, Shane Baskin of Black Box Studios in Charlotte, North Carolina. We've worked together on numerous shoots over the past couple of years and have had a blast each and every time. Shane never stops surprising and impressing me with her innovations and creativity. She does whatever it takes to get the shot we both want and just doesn't quit until it happens.

Universal Yarn and Premier Yarns were the sole suppliers of yarn for the mitts and mittens. Thanks for your generosity and support, Hal and Yonca Ozbelli!

My coworker and friend Katie Ward donated her lovely hands and skills to the tutorial photos in the back of this book. She was a seasoned crocheter before these were shot, but still managed to learn a few new tricks. Katie is a great student and picked up new skills in no time flat. Thank you for your time and patience, Katie!

Contents

Introduction

I am lucky enough to design and write knitting and crochet patterns for a living as part of my job with a yarn company. I also do independent knitting design. If anyone in the fiber world knows me for anything, it is knitting patterns. What most people don't know is that crochet was my first yarny love. I learned to crochet at age twenty to kill time at a pizza-making job. The Internet was still young and I wasn't very savvy at it. Although I learned how to do the basic stitches from a craft store booklet, any techniques that were learned beyond that were "invented" by me. I now know that is completely untrue, of course. Plenty of folks before and after my time "invented" some of the same things—tapestry crochet, mesh stitches, and other stitches I thought were uniquely mine.

Looking back, what I appreciate most about making things up as I went with crochet was that there was no one and nothing to tell me I was doing something wrong. If it made sense or I liked the way it looked, I did it. The most fun was to have an idea, problem solve, and execute that idea. This collection of twenty-five mitts and mittens was approached in much the same way. Last year I did a book of twenty-five knitted mitts and mittens. When approached to do a similar book but for crochet I was initially skeptical that I could come up with twenty-five more ideas for hands. But after some brief pondering, I was reminded that although knitting and crochet have some things in common, there is so much more that is different between the two crafts. To me, crochet is a much freer needlework craft and has the ability to behave in many more interesting ways than knitting. Just take a look at knit and crochet charts side by side. Crochet goes this way and that, stitches can be short or tall. Crochet really knows how to have a good time!

My own personal tastes run the gamut from girly to punk to conservative and everything in between. The projects in this book are intended to be representative of this haberdashery of style. I hope to offer a little something for every crocheter out there.

Lederhosen
for Hands

Be prepared for a German good time with these entertaining mitts. Reminiscent of decorative lederhosen (German breeches), the color changes and simple textured stitches of these mitts keep the work interesting. Made in 100% linen, this pair is great for warmer months. A single row of double crochet mesh on both the back of the hand and the palm provides an extra element of breathability.

FINISHED MEASUREMENTS
Hand circumference: 7¹/₂"/19 cm
Length: 6¹/₄"/16 cm

SIZE
Women's Small

YARN
Fibra Natura Flax, light weight #3 yarn (100% linen; 137 yds/1.75 oz; 125 m/50 g)
• 1 skein #102 Poppy (A)
• 1 skein #15 Black (B)
• 1 skein #04 Pearl (C)

HOOK AND OTHER MATERIALS
• US B-1 (2.25 mm) crochet hook
• Tapestry needle
• Two ³/₄"/2 cm buttons

GAUGE
28 sts x 32 rows in sc = 4"/10 cm square
Be sure to check your gauge!

NOTES

- The hand portion of this mitt is worked in one piece. The back of the hand is worked from the inside out, and the palm is worked from the outside in.
- The cuff is worked separately and sewn to the hand.
- The thumb is worked off the side of the hand and is shaped using short rows. See page 142 for a photo tutorial.

STITCH GUIDE

Double Crochet 3 Together Decrease (dc3tog-dec)
Yo and insert hook into st indicated, yo and pull up a lp (3 lps on hook), yo and pull through 2 lps, [sk next st, yo and insert hook into next st, yo and pull through 2 lps] 2 times, yo and pull through all 4 lps on hook—4 sts dec'd.

Right Mitt

Back of Hand

With A, ch 20.

Row 1 (RS): Hdc in blo of 2nd ch from hook and in blo of next 17 chs, [hdc, ch 1, hdc, ch 1, hdc] in last ch, working along other side of beg ch through blo (free lp), hdc in each of next 18 chs, finishing last hdc with B, turn.

Row 2 (WS): With B, ch 1, fphdc in same hdc, fphdc in next 17 hdc, {[fphdc, ch 1, fphdc] in next hdc} 3 times, fphdc in next 18 hdc, finishing last hdc with C, turn.

Row 3: With C, ch 1, sc in blo of same hdc, sc in blo of next 18 hdc, [sc, ch 1, sc] in next ch-1 sp, sc in blo of next 2 hdc, sc in next ch-1 sp, sc in blo of next 2 hdc, [sc, ch 1, sc] in next ch-1 sp, sc in blo of next 19 hdc, turn.

Back of Hand

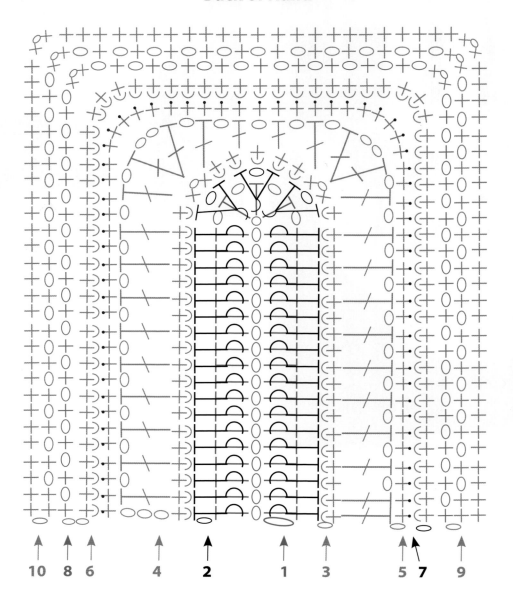

Row 4: Ch 3 (counts as dc), dc in next sc, [ch 1, sk next sc, dc in next sc] 9 times, ch 1, [dc, ch 2, dc] in ch-1 sp, ch 1, dc in next sc, [ch 1, sk next sc, dc in next sc] 3 times, ch 1, [dc, ch 2, dc] in ch-1 sp, [ch 1, sk next sc, dc in next sc] 10 times, dc in last sc, turn—31 dc, 2 ch-2 sps, 25 ch-1 sps.

Row 5: Ch 1, sc in same st, sc in next 21 sts and sps, 5 sc in ch-2 sp, sc in next 11 sts and sps, 5 sc in ch-2 sp, sc in next 22 sts and sps, turn.

Row 6: Ch 1, sc in blo of same st, sc in blo of next 23 sc, 3 sc in blo of next sc, sc in blo of next 15 sc, 3 sc in blo of next sc, sc in blo of next 24 sc, finishing last sc with B, turn.

Row 7: With B, ch 1, working through front (unworked) lp of each sc from Row 5, sl st in each st across, turn. Cut B.

Row 8: With A, ch 2, sc in first sc from Row 6, [ch 1, sk next sc, sc in next sc] 12 times, ch 1, [sc, ch 1, sc] in next sc, ch 1, sc in next sc, [ch 1, sk next sc, sc in next sc] 8 times, ch 1, [sc, ch 1, sc] in next sc, ch 1, sc in next sc, [ch 1, sk next sc, sc in next sc] 12 times, finishing last sc with C, turn. Cut A.

Row 9: Join C, ch 1, sc in same sc, sc in next ch-1 sp, [ch 1, sk next sc, sc in next ch-1 sp] 12 times, ch 1, sk next sc, [sc, ch 1, sc] in next ch-1 sp, [ch 1, sk next sc, sc in next ch-1 sp] 10 times, ch 1, sk next sc, [sc, ch 1, sc] in next ch-1 sp, [ch 1, sk next sc, sc in next ch-1 sp] 13 times, sc in last sc, turn.

Row 10: Ch 1, sc in same sc, sc in next 27 sts and sps, [sc, ch 1, sc] in next ch-1 sp, sc in next 23 sts and sps, [sc, ch 1, sc] in next ch-1 sp, sc in next 28 sts and sps, turn—83 sc, 2 ch-1 sps.

Palm

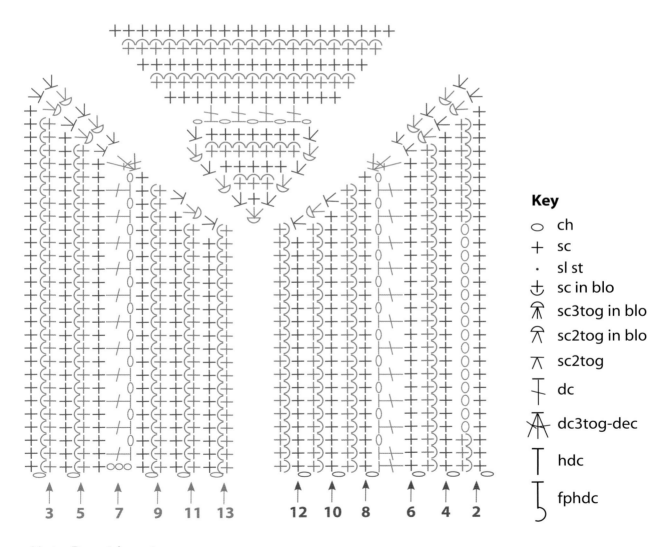

Key

⌒	ch
+	sc
·	sl st
⟊	sc in blo
⟆	sc3tog in blo
⋀	sc2tog in blo
⋀	sc2tog
⊤	dc
⋀	dc3tog-dec
⊤	hdc
⌐	fphdc

Note: Row 1 is not shown on chart

Palm

Note: Palm is worked in C only.

Row 1 (RS): Ch 1, sc in blo of same sc, sc in blo of next 28 sc, sc in blo of next 28 sc, sc in ch-1 sp, ch 25, sk next 25 sc, being careful not to twist ch, sc in next ch-1 sp, sc in blo of next 29 sc, turn—85 sts.

Row 2 (WS): Ch 1, sc in same sc, sc in next 27 sc, sc2tog, working through back lp and bottom bump of each ch and with WS of ch facing, sc2tog (first 2 chs), sc in next 21 chs, sc2tog (last 2 chs), sc2tog (next 2 sc), sc in each of next 28 sc, turn—81 sc.

Row 3: Ch 1, sc in blo of same sc, sc in blo of next 26 sc, [sc2tog in blo] 2 times, sc in blo of next 19 sc, [sc2tog in blo] 2 times, sc in blo of next 8 sc, ch 16 for thumb opening, sk next 16 sc, sc in blo of last 3 sc, turn—77 sts.

Row 4: Ch 1, sc in same sc, sc in next 2 sc, working through back lp and bottom bump of each ch, sc in next 16 chs, sc in next 7 sc, [sc2tog] 2 times, sc in next 17 sc, [sc2tog] 2 times, sc in next 26 sc, turn—73 sc.

Row 5: Ch 1, sc in blo of same sc, sc in blo of next 24 sc, [sc2tog in blo] 2 times, sc in blo of next 15 sc, [sc2tog in blo] 2 times, sc in blo of next 25 sc, turn—69 sc.

Row 6: Ch 1, sc in same sc, sc in next 23 sc, [sc2tog] 2 times, sc in next 13 sc, [sc2tog] 2 times, sc in next 24 sc, turn—65 sc.

Row 7: Ch 3 (counts as dc), dc in next sc, [ch 1, sk next sc, dc in next sc] 10 times, ch 1, sk next sc, dc3tog-dec over next 5 sc (see Stitch Guide), [ch 1, sk next sc, dc in next sc] 4 times, ch 1, sk next sc, dc3tog-dec over next 5 sc, [ch 1, sk next sc, dc in next sc] 11 times, dc in last sc, turn—57 sts.

Row 8: Ch 1, sc in same st, sc in each of next 22 sts and sps, sc2tog (next dc3tog-dec + ch-1 sp), sc in each of next 7 sts and sps, sc2tog (next ch-1 sp + dc3tog-dec), sc in each of next 23 sts and sps, turn—55 sc.

Row 9: Ch 1, sc in blo of same sc, sc in blo of next 21 sc, sc2tog in blo, sc in blo of next 7 sc, sc2tog in blo, sc in blo of next 22 sc, turn—53 sc.

Row 10: Ch 1, sc in same sc, sc in next 19 sc, [sc2tog] 2 times, sc in next 5 sc, [sc2tog] 2 times, sc in next 20 sc, turn—49 sc.

Row 11: Ch 1, sc in blo of same sc, sc in blo of next 18 sc, [sc2tog in blo] 2 times, sc in blo of next 3 sc, [sc2tog in blo only] 2 times, sc in blo of next 19 sc, turn—45 sc.

Row 12: Ch 1, sc in same sc, sc in next 17 sc, [sc2tog] 2 times, sc in next sc, [sc2tog] 2 times, sc in next 18 sc, turn—41 sc.

Row 13: Ch 1, sc in blo of same sc, sc in blo of next 18 sc, sc3tog in blo, sc in blo of next 19 sc—39 sc. Fasten off, leaving 12"/30.5 cm tail. Mattress stitch tog each half of last row worked, working through blo of each sc.

Thumb

With Palm facing up, attach C to top edge of thumb opening.

First Half

Row 1 (RS): Ch 1, sc in blo of same sc and next 13 sc, turn—2 sts left unworked, 14 sc.

Row 2 (WS): Ch 1, sc in each sc to end, turn—14 sc.

Row 3: Ch 1, sc in blo of same sc and next 11 sc, turn.

Row 4: Ch 1, sc in each sc to end, turn—12 sc.

Row 5: Ch 1, sc in blo of same sc and next 8 sc, turn.

Row 6: Ch 1, sc in each sc to end, turn—9 sc.

Row 7: Ch 1, working through blo of each sc, sc in same sc and next 8 sc, [work next sc tog with t-ch-1, sc in next 2 sc, [work next sc tog with t-ch-1, sc in next sc] 2 times, working along other side of thumb opening in free lp of chs, sc in next 16 chs, turn.

Second Half

Row 8: Ch 1, sc in same sc and next 13 sc, turn.

Row 9: Ch 1, sc in blo of each sc to end, turn.

Row 10: Ch 1, sc in same sc and next 11 sc, turn.

Row 11: Ch 1, sc in blo of each sc to end, turn.

Row 12: Ch 1, sc in same sc and next 8 sc, turn.

Row 13: Ch 1, sc in blo of each sc to end, turn.

Row 14: Ch 1, sc in same sc and next 8 sc, [work next sc tog with t-ch-1, sc in next 2 sc, [work next sc tog with t-ch-1, sc in next sc] 2 times; rotate thumb so that the Second Half has the RS facing you, working through blo of each st, sl st last sc from Second Half made tog with the lowest sc from the First Half, sl st rem sc tog up to top opening of thumb.

Rnd 1: Working along top opening of thumb, ch 1, work 9 sc along Second Half, 1 sc in center gap, and 9 sc along First Half.

Rnd 2: Loosely sl st in blo of each sc around. Fasten off.

Top Edging

With Palm facing, attach C to right edge.

Rnd 1: Ch 1, sc in sp bet Palm and Back of Hand, sc in free lp of each ch across, sc in sp bet Palm and Back of Hand, working across Back of Hand, sc in blo of each sc across.

Rnd 2: Loosely sl st in blo of each sc around. Fasten off.

Lower Edging

Attach C with sl st anywhere on lower edge of mitt.

Rnd 1: Ch 1, sc in same st, work 49 more sc evenly around, join with sl st to beg sc.

Rnd 2: Working through blo of each sc, sc around, dec'ing 4 sc evenly—46 sc. Fasten off.

Cuff

With A, ch 49.

Note: Rows 1 and 2 are worked back and forth in joined rows. Rnds 3 and 4 are worked in rnds.

Row 1 (RS): [Hdc, ch 1, hdc, ch 1, hdc] in blo of 2nd ch from hook, hdc in blo of next 46 chs, [hdc, ch 1, hdc, ch 1, hdc] in last ch, working along other side of beg ch through blo (free lp), hdc in next 46 chs, switch to B and join with sl st to beg hdc, turn—98 hdc, 4 ch-1 sps. Cut A.

Row 2 (WS): Ch 1, fphdc in next 46 hdc, {[fphdc, ch 1, fphdc] in next hdc} 3 times, fphdc in next 46 hdc, {[fphdc, ch 1, fphdc] in next hdc} 3 times, join with sl st to beg hdc, turn.

Rnd 3 (RS): Ch 1, [sc in next hdc, 2 sc in next ch, sc in next hdc] 3 times, sc in next 46 hdc, sc in next hdc, 2 sc in next ch, sc in next hdc, ch 4 for buttonhole, sk next [hdc, ch 1, hdc], sc in next hdc, 2 sc in next ch, sc in next hdc, sc in next 46 hdc, join with sl st to beg sc, do not turn.

Rnd 4 (RS): Ch 1, working through blo of each sc, sc in same st, [2 sc in next sc, sc in next 3 sc] 2 times, 2 sc in next sc, sc in next 49 sc, 2 sc in next sc, sc in next 3 sc, 5 sc in ch-4 sp, sc in next sc, 2 sc in next sc, sc in next 48 sc, join with sl st to beg sc. Fasten off.

Attaching Cuff

Lay mitt in front of you, Palm down and Back of Hand facing up, with Lower Edging toward you and Upper Edging facing away. Lay out Cuff with button loop on LH side and other end even with side of mitt. With mattress stitch and B, join Cuff to Lower Edging along all 46 sts of Lower Edging and the right-most 46 sts of straight edge of Cuff, working through back loops only of both Cuff and Lower Edging.

Left Mitt

Top of Hand
Work as for Right Mitt.

Palm

Rows 1–2: Work as for Right Mitt.

Row 3: Ch 1, sc in blo of same sc and next 2 sc, ch 16 for thumb opening, sk next 16 sc, sc in blo of next 8 sc, [sc2tog in blo] 2 times, sc in blo of next 19 sc, [sc2tog in blo] 2 times, sc in blo of next 27 sc, turn.

Row 4: Ch 1, sc in same sc and next 25 sc, [sc2tog] 2 times, sc in next 17 sc, [sc2tog] 2 times, sc in next 7 sc, working through back lp and bottom bump of each ch, sc in next 16 chs, sc in last 3 sc, turn.

Rows 5–13: Work as for Right Mitt.

Thumb

Join C to top edge of thumb opening.

First Half

Row 1 (RS): Ch 1, working through free lp of chs, sc in same ch and next 13 chs, turn—2 sts left unworked.

Row 2 (WS): Ch 1, sc in each sc to end, turn—14 sc.

Row 3: Ch 1, sc in blo of same sc and next 11 sc, turn.

Row 4: Ch 1, sc in each sc to end, turn—12 sc.

Row 5: Ch 1, sc in blo of same sc and next 8 sc, turn.

Row 6: Ch 1, sc in each sc to end, turn—9 sc.

Row 7: Ch 1, working through blo of each sc, sc in same sc and next 8 sc, [work next sc tog with t-ch-1, sc in next 2 sc, [work next sc tog with t-ch-1, sc in next sc] 2 times, working along other side of thumb opening, sc in blo of next 16 sc, turn.

Second Half

Row 8: Ch 1, sc in same sc and next 13 sc, turn.

Row 9: Ch 1, sc in blo of each sc to end, turn.

Row 10: Ch 1, sc in same sc and next 11 sc, turn.

Row 11: Ch 1, sc in blo of each sc to end, turn.

Row 12: Ch 1, sc in same sc and next 8 sc, turn.

Row 13: Ch 1, sc in blo of each sc to end, turn.

Row 14: Ch 1, sc in same sc and next 8 sc, [work next sc tog with t-ch-1, sc in next 2 sc, [work next sc tog with t-ch-1, sc in next sc] 2 times; rotate thumb so that the Second Half has the RS facing you, working through blo of each st, sl st last sc from Second Half made tog with the lowest sc from the First Half, sl st rem sc tog up to top opening of thumb.

Rnd 1: Working along top opening of thumb, ch 1, work 9 sc along Second Half, 1 sc in center gap, and 9 sc along First Half.

Rnd 2: Loosely sl st in blo of each sc around. Fasten off.

Lower Edging

Work as for Right Mitt.

Cuff

Work as for Right Mitt.

Attaching Cuff

Lay mitt in front of you, Palm down and Back of Hand facing up, with Lower Edging toward you and Upper Edging facing away. Lay out Cuff with button loop on the RH side and other end even with side of mitt. With mattress stitch and B, join Cuff to Lower Edging along all 46 sts of Lower Edging and the right-most 46 sts of straight edge of Cuff, working through back loops only of both Cuff and Lower Edging.

Finishing

Weave in ends and wet-block. Try on mitt and fold over button loop to determine best place for button. Sew button to Cuff beneath button loop.

> **TIP:** Experiment with color in this mitt. Lederhosen would look great in just one color or many more!

Trellis Climb

A simple double crochet mesh forms the trellis-like foundation for these adorable mitts. The flower, leaf, and stem are crocheted separately and sewn on as appliqués, leaving loads of room for creativity. Try your hand at designing your own flower or play around with the placement of the stem. The possibilities are endless!

FINISHED MEASUREMENTS
Hand circumference: 7$\frac{1}{4}$ (8$\frac{3}{4}$, 9$\frac{3}{4}$)"/18.5 (22, 25) cm
Length: 6$\frac{3}{4}$ (7$\frac{1}{4}$, 7$\frac{1}{2}$)"/17 (18.5, 19) cm

SIZES
Women's Small (Medium, Large)
Shown in Small.

YARN
Premier Yarns Afternoon Cotton, light weight #3 yarn (100% Egyptian Giza mercerized cotton; 136 yds/1.75 oz; 125 m/50 g)
• 1 (2, 2) ball(s) #23-08 Butter Cream (MC)
• 1 ball #23-04 New Leaf (CC1)
• 1 ball #22-02 True Red (CC2)

HOOK AND OTHER MATERIALS
- US B-1 (2.25 mm) crochet hook
- Tapestry needle
- Sewing needle
- Sewing thread to match MC
- Straight pins

GAUGE
25 sts x 12 rows in Double Crochet Mesh patt = 4"/10 cm square
Be sure to check your gauge!

NOTES
- This mitt is worked from the cuff up in joined rows.
- The leaves and flowers are made using an adjustable ring; for a photo tutorial, see page 123.

STITCH GUIDE
V-st
[Dc, ch 1, dc] in sp indicated.
Picot
[Sl st, ch 3, sl st] in st indicated.
Beg Picot
[Ch 3, sl st] in st indicated.

STITCH PATTERN
Double Crochet Mesh (even number of sts)
Set-up row: Ch 4 (counts as dc + ch 1), sk next sc, [dc in next dc, ch 1, sk next sc] across, join with sl st to third ch of beg ch-4, turn.
Row 1: Sl st in next ch-1 sp, ch 4 (counts as dc + ch 1), sk next dc, [dc in next ch-1 sp, ch 1, sk next dc] across, join with sl st to 3rd ch of beg ch-4, turn.
Rep Row 1 for patt.

Right Mitt

Cuff
With MC, ch 44 (52, 60). Join with sl st through both top lp and bottom bump of first ch to form ring.
Rnd 1 (RS): Ch 1, sc in same st, sc through both top lp and bottom bump of each ch around, join with sl st to beg sc—44 (52, 60) sc.
Row 2 (RS): Work Set-up row of Double Crochet Mesh patt—22 (26, 30) dc, 22 (26, 30) ch-1 sps.
Row 3: Work Row 1 of Double Crochet Mesh patt.
Rows 4–5: Work Double Crochet Mesh patt.

Thumb Gusset
Row 1 (RS): Sl st in next ch-1 sp, ch 4 (counts as dc + ch 1), sk next dc, [dc in next ch-1 sp, ch 1, sk next dc] 17 (20, 23) times, v-st in next ch-1 sp, ch 1, [dc in next ch-1 sp, ch 1, sk next dc] 3 (4, 5) times, join with sl st to 3rd ch of beg ch-4, turn—2 sts inc'd.

Row 2 (WS): Sl st in next ch-1 sp, ch 4 (counts as dc + ch 1), sk next dc, [dc in next ch-1 sp, ch 1, sk next dc] 3 (4, 5) times, v-st in ch-1 sp of next v-st, [dc in next ch-1 sp, ch 1, sk next dc] 18 (21, 24) times, join with sl st to 3rd ch of beg ch-4, turn—2 sts inc'd.
Row 3: Sl st in next ch-1 sp, ch 4 (counts as dc + ch 1), sk next dc, [dc in next ch-1 sp, ch 1, sk next dc] 18 (21, 24) times, v-st in ch-1 sp of next v-st, [dc in next ch-1 sp, ch 1, sk next dc] 4 (5, 6) times, join with sl st to 3rd ch of beg ch-4, turn—2 sts inc'd.
Row 4: Sl st in next ch-1 sp, ch 4 (counts as dc + ch 1), sk next dc, [dc in next ch-1 sp, ch 1, sk next dc] 4 (5, 6) times, v-st in ch-1 sp of next v-st, [dc in next ch-1 sp, ch 1, sk next dc] 19 (22, 25) times, join with sl st to 3rd ch of beg ch-4, turn—2 sts inc'd.
Row 5: Sl st in next ch-1 sp, ch 4 (counts as dc + ch 1), sk next dc, [dc in next ch-1 sp, ch 1, sk next dc] 19 (22, 25) times, v-st in ch-1 sp of next v-st, [dc in next ch-1 sp, ch 1, sk next dc] 5 (6, 7) times, join with sl st to 3rd ch of beg ch-4, turn—2 sts inc'd.
Row 6: Sl st in next ch-1 sp, ch 4 (counts as dc + ch 1), sk next dc, [dc in next ch-1 sp, ch 1, sk next dc] 5 (6, 7) times, v-st in ch-1 sp of next v-st, [dc in next ch-1 sp, ch 1, sk next dc] 20 (23, 26) times, join with sl st to third ch of beg ch-4, turn—2 sts inc'd.
Row 7: Sl st in next ch-1 sp, ch 4 (counts as dc + ch 1), sk next dc, [dc in next ch-1 sp, ch 1, sk next dc] 20 (23, 26) times, v-st in ch-1 sp of next v-st, [dc in next ch-1 sp, ch 1, sk next dc] 6 (7, 8) times, join with sl st to 3rd ch of beg ch-4, turn—2 sts inc'd.
Row 8: Sl st in next ch-1 sp, ch 4 (counts as dc + ch 1), sk next dc, [dc in next ch-1 sp, ch 1, sk next dc] 6 (7, 8) times, v-st in ch-1 sp of next v-st, [dc in next ch-1 sp, ch 1, sk next dc] 21 (24, 27) times, join with sl st to 3rd ch of beg ch-4, turn—2 sts inc'd.

Small Size Only
Row 9: Sl st in next ch-1 sp, ch 4 (counts as dc + ch 1), sk next dc, [dc in next ch-1 sp, ch 1, sk next dc] 16 times, v-st in next ch-1 sp, ch 1, sk next 19 sts, v-st in next ch-1 sp, [dc in next ch-1 sp, ch 1, sk next dc] 2 times, join with sl st to 3rd ch of beg ch-4, turn—46 sts.

Medium Size Only
Row 9: Sl st in next ch-1 sp, ch 4 (counts as dc + ch 1), sk next dc, [dc in next ch-1 sp, ch 1, sk next dc] 24 times, v-st in ch-1 sp of next v-st, [dc in next ch-1 sp, ch 1, sk next dc] 8 times, join with sl st to 3rd ch of beg ch-4, turn—2 sts inc'd.
Row 10: Sl st in next ch-1 sp, ch 4 (counts as dc + ch 1), sk next dc, [dc in next ch-1 sp, ch 1, sk next dc] 2 times, v-st in next ch-1 sp, sk next 21 sts, v-st in next ch-1 sp, [dc in next ch-1 sp, ch 1, sk next dc] 20 times, join with sl st to 3rd ch of beg ch-4, turn—54 sts.

Large Size Only

Row 9: Sl st in next ch-1 sp, ch 4 (counts as dc + ch 1), sk next dc, [dc in next ch-1 sp, ch 1, sk next dc] 27 times, v-st in ch-1 sp of next v-st, [dc in next ch-1 sp, ch 1, sk next dc] 9 times, join with sl st to third ch of beg ch-4, turn—2 sts inc'd.

Row 10: Sl st in next ch-1 sp, ch 4 (counts as dc + ch 1), sk next dc, [dc in next ch-1 sp, ch 1, sk next dc] 9 times, v-st in ch-1 sp of next v-st, [dc in next ch-1 sp, ch 1, sk next dc] 28 times, join with sl st to 3rd ch of beg ch-4, turn—2 sts inc'd.

Row 11: Sl st in next ch-1 sp, ch 4 (counts as dc + ch 1), sk next dc, [dc in next ch-1 sp, ch 1, sk next dc] 22 times, v-st in next ch-1 sp, sk next 23 sts, v-st in next ch-1 sp, [dc in next ch-1 sp, ch 1, sk next dc] 4 times, join with sl st to 3rd ch of beg ch-4, turn—62 sts.

Upper Hand

All Sizes

Work in Double Crochet Mesh patt for 4 rows. Small and Large sizes do not need to turn. Medium size needs to turn so RS is facing.

Next rnd (RS): Beg picot in same st, picot in next dc and each dc around, join with sl st to beg st. Fasten off.

Lower Edging

Join MC with sl st to beg-ch edge at seam, through unworked lp of ch.

Rnd 1 (RS): Beg picot in same ch, skip next ch, [picot in next ch, skip next ch] around, join with sl st in same st as beg picot. Fasten off.

Thumb

Join MC to center of Thumb gap.

Rnd 1 (RS): Ch 1, work 3 sc along first half of gap, sc in each of next 19 (21, 23) sts and chs, work 2 sc along second half of gap, join with sl st to beg sc—24 (26, 28) sc.

Rnd 2: Ch 1, beg picot in same sc, skip next sc, [picot in next sc, skip next sc] around, join with sl st to beg sc. Fasten off.

Left Mitt

Work as for Right Mitt to Thumb Gusset.

Thumb Gusset

Row 1 (RS): Sl st in next ch-1 sp, ch 4 (counts as dc + ch 1), sk next dc, [dc in next ch-1 sp, ch 1, sk next dc] 2 (3, 4) times, v-st in next ch-1 sp, ch 1, [dc in next ch-1 sp, ch 1, sk next dc] 18 (21, 24) times, join with sl st to 3rd ch of beg ch-4, turn—2 sts inc'd.

Row 2 (WS): Sl st in next ch-1 sp, ch 4 (counts as dc + ch 1), sk next dc, [dc in next ch-1 sp, ch 1, sk next dc] 18 (21, 24) times, v-st in ch-1 sp of next v-st, [dc in next ch-1 sp, ch 1, sk next dc] 3 (4, 5) times, join with sl st to 3rd ch of beg ch-4, turn—2 sts inc'd.

Row 3: Sl st in next ch-1 sp, ch 4 (counts as dc + ch 1), sk next dc, [dc in next ch-1 sp, ch 1, sk next dc] 3 (4, 5) times, v-st in next ch-1 sp, ch 1, [dc in next ch-1 sp, ch 1, sk next dc] 19 (22, 25) times, join with sl st to 3rd ch of beg ch-4, turn—2 sts inc'd.

Row 4: Sl st in next ch-1 sp, ch 4 (counts as dc + ch 1), sk next dc, [dc in next ch-1 sp, ch 1, sk next dc] 19 (22, 25) times, v-st in ch-1 sp of next v-st, [dc in next ch-1 sp, ch 1, sk next dc] 4 (5, 6) times, join with sl st to 3rd ch of beg ch-4, turn—2 sts inc'd.

Row 5: Sl st in next ch-1 sp, ch 4 (counts as dc + ch 1), sk next dc, [dc in next ch-1 sp, ch 1, sk next dc] 4 (5, 6) times, v-st in next ch-1 sp, ch 1, [dc in next ch-1 sp, ch 1, sk next dc] 20 (23, 26) times, join with sl st to 3rd ch of beg ch-4, turn—2 sts inc'd.

Row 6: Sl st in next ch-1 sp, ch 4 (counts as dc + ch 1), sk next dc, [dc in next ch-1 sp, ch 1, sk next dc] 20 (23, 26) times, v-st in ch-1 sp of next v-st, [dc in next ch-1 sp, ch 1, sk next dc] 5 (6, 7) times, join with sl st to 3rd ch of beg ch-4, turn—2 sts inc'd.

Row 7: Sl st in next ch-1 sp, ch 4 (counts as dc + ch 1), sk next dc, [dc in next ch-1 sp, ch 1, sk next dc] 5 (6, 7) times, v-st in next ch-1 sp, ch 1, [dc in next ch-1 sp, ch 1, sk next dc] 21 (24, 27) times, join with sl st to 3rd ch of beg ch-4, turn—2 sts inc'd.

Row 8: Sl st in next ch-1 sp, ch 4 (counts as dc + ch 1), sk next dc, [dc in next ch-1 sp, ch 1, sk next dc] 21 (24, 27) times, v-st in ch-1 sp of next v-st, [dc in next ch-1 sp, ch 1, sk next dc] 6 (7, 8) times, join with sl st to 3rd ch of beg ch-4, turn—2 sts inc'd.

Small Size Only

Row 9: Sl st in next ch-1 sp, ch 4 (counts as dc + ch 1), sk next dc, dc in next ch-1 sp, ch 1, sk next dc, v-st in next ch-1 sp, ch 1, sk next 19 sts, v-st in next ch-1 sp, [dc in next ch-1 sp, ch 1, sk next dc] 17 times, join with sl st to 3rd ch of beg ch-4, turn—46 sts.

Medium Size Only

Row 9: Sl st in next ch-1 sp, ch 4 (counts as dc + ch 1), sk next dc, [dc in next ch-1 sp, ch 1, sk next dc] 7 times, v-st in next ch-1 sp, ch 1, [dc in next ch-1 sp, ch 1, sk next dc] 25 times, join with sl st to 3rd ch of beg ch-4, turn—2 sts inc'd.

Row 10: Sl st in next ch-1 sp, ch 4 (counts as dc + ch 1), sk next dc, [dc in next ch-1 sp, ch 1, sk next dc] 19 times, v-st in next ch-1 sp, sk next 21 sts, v-st in next ch-1 sp, [dc in next ch-1 sp, ch 1, sk next dc] 3 times, join with sl st to 3rd ch of beg ch-4, turn—54 sts.

Large Size Only

Row 9: Sl st in next ch-1 sp, ch 4 (counts as dc + ch 1), sk next dc, [dc in next ch-1 sp, ch 1, sk next dc] 8 times, v-st in next ch-1 sp, ch 1, [dc in next ch-1 sp, ch 1, sk next dc] 28 times, join with sl st to 3rd ch of beg ch-4 turn—2 sts inc'd.

Row 10: Sl st in next ch-1 sp, ch 4 (counts as dc + ch 1), sk next dc, [dc in next ch-1 sp, ch 1, sk next dc] 28 times, v-st in ch-1 sp of next v-st, [dc in next ch-1 sp, ch 1, sk next dc] 9 times, join with sl st to 3rd ch of beg ch-4, turn—2 sts inc'd.

Row 11: Sl st in next ch-1 sp, ch 4 (counts as dc + ch 1), sk next dc, [dc in next ch-1 sp, ch 1, sk next dc] 3 times, v-st in next ch-1 sp, sk next 23 sts, v-st in next ch-1 sp, [dc in next ch-1 sp, ch 1, sk next dc] 23 times, join with sl st to 3rd ch of beg ch-4, turn—62 sts.

Complete remainder of Left Mitt as for Right Mitt.

Finishing

Stem (make 2; 1 per mitt)
With CC1, ch 40.
Row 1: Working through bottom bump of each ch, sl st in 2nd ch from hook and each ch across. Fasten off. Weave in ends.

Leaf (make 2; 1 per mitt)
With CC1, begin with adjustable ring.
Rnd 1: Ch 1, into ring work [3 sc, 2 hdc, dc, ch 1, dc, 2 hdc, 3 sc], join with sl st to beg sc. Fasten off. Weave in ends.

Flower (make 2; 1 per mitt)
With MC, beg with adjustable ring.
Rnd 1: Ch 1, work 6 sc in ring, with CC2, join with sl st to form ring. Cut MC.
Rnd 2: With CC2, [ch 3, working through both bottom bump and back lp, sl st in 2nd ch from hook and in next ch (small petal made), sl st in same sc, ch 5, sl st in 2nd ch from hook and next 3 chs (large petal made), sl st in next sc] 6 times. Fasten off. Weave in ends.

Pin Stem, Leaf, and Flower to each mitt, using photos as a placement guide. With sewing needle and thread, invisibly sew pieces to mitt.

Overpass Mittens

Cousin to Underpass Mittens (page 17), this pair works well for both ladies and gentlemen. Its super-long cuffs can be worn up or down. Folded up, the cuff provides an extra layer of insulation from frigid winter weather. The top of this textured mitten is shaped while staying in pattern, looking totally professional. Can't decide whether to go Over or Under? Don't—make both!

SIZES
Women's Small (Medium, Large)/Men's Extra Small (Small, Medium)
Shown in Women's Medium/Men's Small.

YARN
Universal Yarn Deluxe DK Superwash, light weight #3 yarn (100% superwash wool; 284 yds/3.5 oz; 260 m/100 g); yarn below is enough to make any size
- 2 balls #815 Teal Viper (MC)
- 1 ball #830 Steel Cut Oats (CC)
Note: If you make both Underpass and Overpass Mittens as shown, only two balls total of each color is needed. The contrast trim for each pair of mittens requires only a small amount of yarn.

FINISHED MEASUREMENTS
Hand circumference: 7 (8^3/$_4$, 10^1/$_2$)"/18 (22, 26.5) cm
Length: 12^1/$_4$ (13^1/$_4$, 14^1/$_4$)"/31 (33.5, 36) cm (with cuff unfolded)

HOOKS AND OTHER MATERIALS

- US E-4 (3.5 mm) crochet hook
- US F-5 (3.75 mm) crochet hook
- Tapestry needle

GAUGE

Using smaller hook, 22 sts x 23 rows in blo sc = 4"/10 cm square

Using larger hook, 18 sts x 18 rnds in Over and Out patt = 4"/10 cm square

Be sure to check your gauge!

NOTES

- The cuff is worked sideways and seamed.
- The hand is worked upward from the side of the cuff.

STITCH GUIDE

Double Crochet-Front Post Double Crochet Decrease (dc-fpdc dec)

Yo and insert hook into next dc, yo and pull through (3 lps on hook), yo and pull through 2 lps (2 lps on hook), yo and insert hook around post of next dc from 2 rows below, yo and pull through (4 lps on hook), yo and pull through 2 lps (3 lps on hook), yo and pull through rem 3 lps, sk dc behind st just made—1 st dec'd.

STITCH PATTERN

Over and Out (multiple of 4 sts)

Row 1 (RS): Ch 1, [fpdc around sc from 2 rows below, sk sc behind fpdc just made, dc in next sc] across, join with sl st to beg dc, turn.

Row 2 (WS): Ch 1, sc in each dc across, join with sl st to beg sc, turn.

Row 3: Ch 1, dc in same sc, fpdc around next dc from 2 rows below (between fpdcs), sk sc behind fpdc just made, [dc in next sc, fpdc around next dc from 2 rows below, sk sc behind fpdc just made] across, join with sl st to beg sc, turn.

Row 4: Ch 1, sc in each dc across, join with sl st to beg sc, turn.

Row 5: Ch 1, [fpdc around dc from 2 rows below (between fpdcs), sk sc behind fpdc just made, dc in next sc] across, join with sl st to beg dc, turn.

Row 6: Ch 1, sc in each dc across, join with sl st to beg sc, turn.

Rep Rows 3–6 for patt.

Right Mitt

With smaller hook and MC, ch 31.

Cuff

Row 1 (RS): Sc in blo of 2nd ch from hook and each ch across—30 sc.

Row 2: Ch 1, sc in blo of each sc across, turn.

[Rep Row 2] 30 (38, 46) times. Break yarn, leaving 16"/40.5 cm tail. Join last row worked tog with beg ch edge using mattress stitch, working through blo of last row worked and both free lps of beg ch edge.

Hand

With larger hook and RS facing, join yarn to seam.

Note: Hand is worked in joined rows.

Set-up row 1 (RS): Ch 1, work 32 (40, 48) sc evenly along edge of Cuff, join with sl st to beg sc.

Set-up row 2 (WS): Ch 1, sc in each sc around, join with sl st to beg sc, turn.

Work Rows 1–6 of Over and Out patt, then rep Rows 3–6.

Thumb Opening

Row 1 (RS): Ch 1, dc in same sc, fpdc around next dc from 2 rows below (between fpdcs), sk sc behind fpdc just made, [dc in next sc, fpdc around next dc from 2 rows below, sk sc behind fpdc just made] 10 (14, 18) times, ch 8, sk next 8 sc, dc in next sc, fpdc around next dc from 2 rows below, join with sl st to beg dc, turn.

Row 2 (WS): Ch 1, sc in each dc and ch across, join with sl st to beg sc.

Row 3: Ch 1, [fpdc around dc from 2 rows below (between fpdcs), skip sc behind fpdc just made, dc in next sc] 11 (15, 19) times, dc in next 8 sc, fpdc around dc from 2 rows below, sk sc behind fpdc just made, dc in next sc, join with sl st to beg dc, turn.

Row 4: Ch 1, sc in each dc across, join with sl st to beg sc.

Upper Hand

Work Rows 3–6 of Over and Out patt 2 (3, 4) times.

Shape Top

Row 1 (RS): Work Row 3 of Over and Out patt over 6 (8, 10) sts, [dc2tog, sk next sc, fpdc around next dc from 2 rows below, sk dc behind fpdc just made], work in patt over next 12 (16, 20) sts, rep from [to] 1 time, work in patt over rem 6 (8, 10) sts, join with sl st to beg dc, turn—28 (36, 44) sts.

Row 2 (WS): Ch 1, sc in each dc across, join with sl st to beg sc, turn.

Row 3: Work Row 5 of Over and Out patt over 5 (7, 9) sts, [dc2tog, sk next sc, fpdc around next dc from 2 rows below, sk dc behind fpdc just made], work in patt over 10 (14, 18) sts, rep from [to] 1 time, work in patt over rem 5 (7, 9) sts, join with sl st to beg dc, turn—24 (32, 40) sts.

Row 4: Ch 1, sc in each dc across, join with sl st to beg sc, turn.

Row 5: Work Row 3 of Over and Out patt over 4 (6, 8) sts, [dc2tog, sk next sc, fpdc around next dc from 2 rows below, sk dc behind fpdc just made], work in patt over 8 (12, 16) sts, rep from [to] 1 time, work in patt over rem 4 (6, 8) sts, join with sl st to beg dc, turn—20 (28, 36) sts.

Row 6: Ch 1, sc in each dc across, join with sl st to beg sc, turn.

Row 7: Work Row 5 of Over and Out patt over 3 (5, 7) sts, [dc2tog, sk next sc, fpdc around next dc from 2 rows below, sk dc behind fpdc just made], work in patt over 6 (10, 14) sts, rep from [to] 1 time, work in patt over rem 3 (5, 7) sts, join with sl st to beg dc, turn—16 (24, 32) sts.

Row 8: Ch 1, sc in first 2 (4, 6) dc, [sc2tog] 2 times, sc in next 4 (8, 12) dc, [sc2tog] 2 times, sc in last 2 (4, 6) sc, join with sl st to beg sc—12 (20, 28) sts.

Row 9: Ch 1, [dc-fpdc dec] across, turn—6 (10, 14) sts.

Row 10: Ch 1, sc in each dc across, join with sl st to beg sc.

Fasten off, leaving 8"/20.5 cm tail. Turn Mitten inside out. Whipstitch last rnd of sc tog through blo of each sc. Draw taut, weave in tail.

Thumb

Join MC to right side of Thumb opening, leaving 8"/20.5 cm tail.

Row 1 (RS): Ch 3 (counts as dc), fpdc around post of next dc from 2 rows below, sk sc behind dc just made, [dc in next dc, fpdc around post of next dc from 2 rows below, sk sc behind dc just made] 3 times, working along upper edge of Thumb opening, [dc in next dc, fpdc around post of next dc from 2 rows below, sk st behind dc just made] 4 times, join with sl st to beg dc, turn—16 sts.

Rows 2–12: Work Rows 4–6 of Over and Out patt 1 time, then rep Rows 3–6 of patt 2 times.

Row 13: [Dc-fpdc dec] across, join with sl st to beg dc—8 sts.

Row 14: Ch 1, sc in each dc across, join with sl st to beg sc.

Fasten off, leaving 6"/15 cm tail. Turn Thumb inside out. Whipstitch last rnd of sc tog through blo of each sc. Draw taut, weave in tail. Close up holes on sides of Thumb using beg tail.

Left Mitten

Work as for Right Mitten to Thumb Opening.

Thumb Opening

Row 1 (RS): Ch 1, dc in same sc, fpdc around next dc from 2 rows below (between fpdcs), sk sc behind fpdc just made, ch 8, sk next 8 sc, [dc in next sc, fpdc around next dc from 2 rows below, sk sc behind fpdc just made] 11 (15, 19) times, join with sl st to beg dc, turn.

Row 2: Ch 1, sc in each dc and ch across, join with sl st to beg sc.

Row 3: Ch 1, fpdc around dc from 2 rows below (between fpdcs), skip sc behind fpdc just made, dc in next sc, dc in each of next 8 sc, [fpdc around dc from 2 rows below (between fpdcs), skip sc behind fpdc just made, dc in next sc] 11 (15, 19) times, join with sl st to beg dc, turn.

Row 4: Ch 1, sc in each dc and ch across, join with sl st to beg sc.

Upper Hand, Shape Top, Thumb

Work as for Right Mitten.

Finishing

Attach CC to beg-ch edge of Cuff. With larger hook and WS facing, loosely sl st in each ch around, fasten off. Weave in rem ends. Fold up cuff to wear.

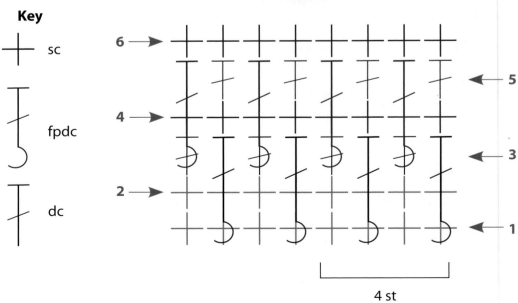

Over and Out Pattern

Key

sc

fpdc

dc

4 st repeat

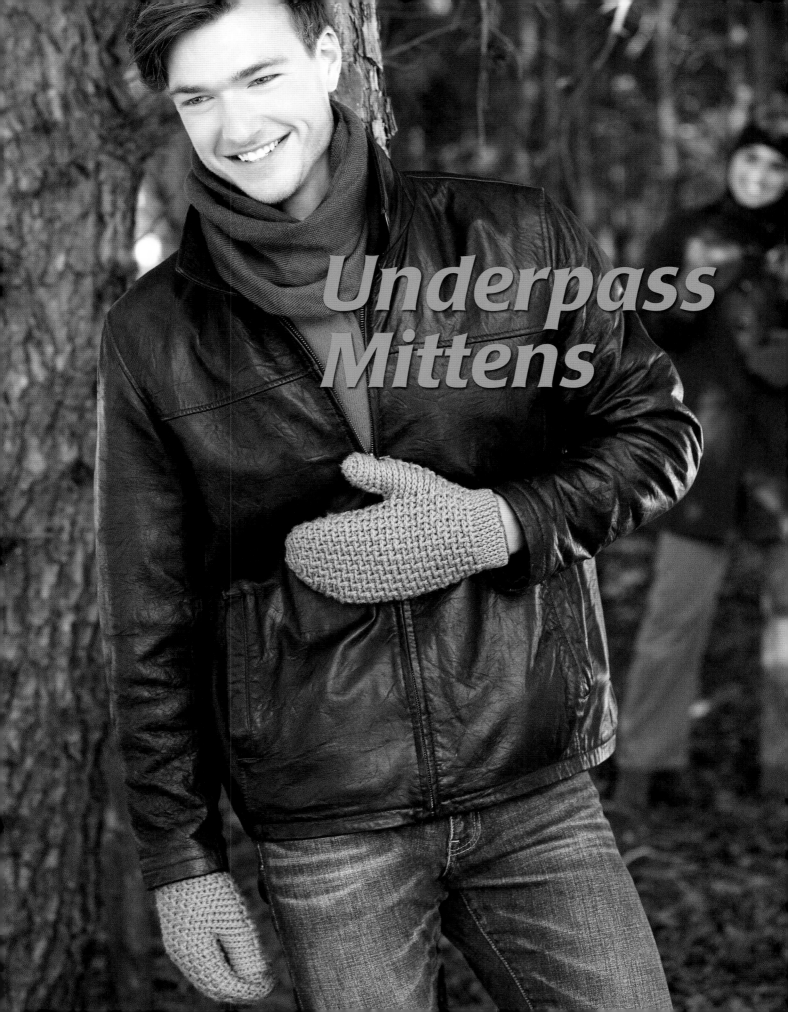

Underpass
Mittens

Pining for a perfectly cozy, snuggly pair of mittens? Look no further. These mittens are worked entirely in post stitches, creating a dense yet lightweight fabric that's going to shield you from the winter-cold blues. The basketweave pattern with its two-row repeat is easy to memorize, allowing you to focus your precious brain cells on other things while you crochet—like planning the awesome snowball fort you're going to build wearing these babies! The cousin to Overpass Mittens (page 13), these are equally suited for guys or gals. This pair is worked in one piece and features a thumb gusset.

FINISHED MEASUREMENTS
Hand circumference: $8^3/_4$ ($10^1/_2$)"/22 (26.5) cm
Length: 9 (10)"/23 (25.5) cm

SIZES
Women's Medium (Large)/Men's Small (Medium)
Shown in Women's Medium/Men's Small.

YARN
Universal Yarn Deluxe DK Superwash, light weight #3 yarn (100% superwash wool; 284 yds/3.5 oz; 260 m/100 g)
• 2 balls #830 Steel Cut Oats (MC)
• 1 ball #815 Teal Viper (CC)
Note: If you make both Underpass and Overpass Mittens as shown, only two balls total of each color is needed. The contrast trim for each pair of mittens requires only a small amount of yarn.

HOOKS AND OTHER MATERIALS
• US E-4 (3.5 mm) crochet hook
• US F-5 (3.75 mm) crochet hook
• Tapestry needle
• 2 removable stitch markers

GAUGE

Using smaller hook, 20 sts x 20 rows in fpdc = 4"/10 cm square

Using larger hook, 18 sts x 16 rnds in Basketweave patt = 4"/10 cm square

Be sure to check your gauge!

STITCH GUIDE

Back Post Double Crochet 2 Together (bpdc2tog)

Yo, insert hook from back around post of next dc, yo and pull up lp (3 lps on hook), yo, insert hook from back around post of next dc, yo and pull up lp (5 lps on hook), [yo and pull through 3 lps on hook] 2 times—1 st dec'd.

STITCH PATTERN

Basketweave (multiple of 4 sts)

Rnd 1: Ch 1, fpdc around same dc, [bpdc around each of next 3 dc, fpdc around next dc] around to last 3 sts, bpdc around each of last 3 dc, join with sl st around post of beg fpdc.

Rnd 2: Ch 1, bpdc around same dc, [bpdc around next dc, fpdc around next dc, bpdc around each of next 2 dc] around to last 3 sts, bpdc around next dc, fpdc around next dc, bpdc around last dc, join with sl st around post of beg bpdc.

Rep Rnds 1–2 for patt.

Right Mitten

With smaller hook and MC, ch 40 (48). Join with sl st in bottom bump of 1st ch to form ring, being careful not to twist chs.

Cuff

Rnd 1: Ch 3 (counts as dc), dc in bump of next ch and bump of each ch around, join with sl st around post of beg dc—40 (48) dc.

Rnd 2: Ch 1, fpdc around same dc and each dc around, join with sl st around post of beg fpdc.

Rnds 3–6: Rep Rnd 2.

Hand

Switch to larger hook.

Work Rnds 1–2 of Basketweave patt.

Thumb Gusset

Rnd 1: Ch 1, fpdc around same dc, [bpdc around each of next 3 dc, fpdc around next dc] 7 (8) times, bpdc around each of next 2 dc, 2 bpdc around next dc, fpdc around next dc, 2 bpdc around next dc, bpdc around each of next 2 dc, [fpdc around next dc, bpdc around each of next 3 dc] 1 (2) times, join with sl st around post of beg fpdc—2 sts inc'd, 42 (50) sts.

Rnd 2: Ch 1, bpdc around same dc, bpdc around next dc, [fpdc around next dc, bpdc around next 3 dc] 7 (8) times, fpdc around next dc, [bpdc around next dc, 2 bpdc around next dc] 2 times, bpdc around next dc, [fpdc around next dc, bpdc around each of next 3 dc] 1 (2) times, fpdc around next dc, bpdc around last dc, join with sl st around post of beg bpdc—2 sts inc'd, 44 (52) sts.

Rnd 3: Ch 1, fpdc around same dc, [bpdc around each of next 3 dc, fpdc around next dc] 7 (8) times, bpdc around each of next 4 dc, 2 bpdc around next dc, fpdc around next dc, 2 bpdc around next dc, bpdc around each of next 4 dc, [fpdc around next dc, bpdc around each of next 3 dc] 1 (2) times, join with sl st around post of beg fpdc—2 sts inc'd, 46 (54) sts.

Rnd 4: Ch 1, bpdc around same dc, bpdc around next dc, [fpdc around next dc, bpdc around next 3 dc] 7 (8) times, fpdc around next dc, bpdc around each of next 3 dc, 2 bpdc around next dc, bpdc around next dc, 2 bpdc around next dc, bpdc around next 3 dc, [fpdc around next dc, bpdc around each of next 3 dc] 1 (2) times, fpdc around next dc, bpdc around last dc, join with sl st around post of beg bpdc—2 sts inc'd, 48 (56) sts.

Rnd 5: Ch 1, fpdc around same dc, [bpdc around each of next 3 dc, fpdc around next dc] 7 (8) times, bpdc around each of next 6 dc, 2 bpdc around next dc, fpdc around next dc, 2 bpdc around next dc, bpdc around next 6 dc, [fpdc around next dc, bpdc around next 3 dc] 1 (2) times, join with sl st around post of beg fpdc—2 sts inc'd, 50 (58) sts.

Rnd 6: Ch 1, bpdc around same dc, bpdc around next dc, [fpdc around next dc, bpdc around next 3 dc] 7 (8) times, fpdc around next dc, bpdc around each of next 5 dc, 2 bpdc around next dc, bpdc around next dc, 2 bpdc around next dc, bpdc around each of next 5 dc, [fpdc around next dc, bpdc around each of next 3 dc] 1 (2) times, fpdc around next dc, bpdc around last dc, join with sl st around post of beg bpdc—2 sts inc'd, 52 (60) sts.

Rnd 7: Ch 1, fpdc around same dc, [bpdc around next 3 dc, fpdc around next dc] 7 (8) times, bpdc around each of next 8 dc, 2 bpdc around next dc, fpdc around next dc, 2 bpdc around next dc, bpdc around each of next 8 dc, [fpdc around next dc, bpdc around each of next 3 dc] 1 (2) times, join with sl st around post of beg fpdc—2 sts inc'd, 54 (62) sts.

Rnd 8: Ch 1, bpdc around same dc, bpdc around next dc, [fpdc around next dc, bpdc around next 3 dc] 7 (8) times, fpdc around next dc, bpdc around each of next 7 dc, 2 bpdc around next dc, bpdc around next dc, 2 bpdc around next dc, bpdc around each of next 7 dc, [fpdc around next dc, bpdc around each of next 3 dc] 1 (2) times, fpdc around next dc, bpdc around last dc, join with sl st around post of beg bpdc—2 sts inc'd, 56 (64) sts.

Basketweave

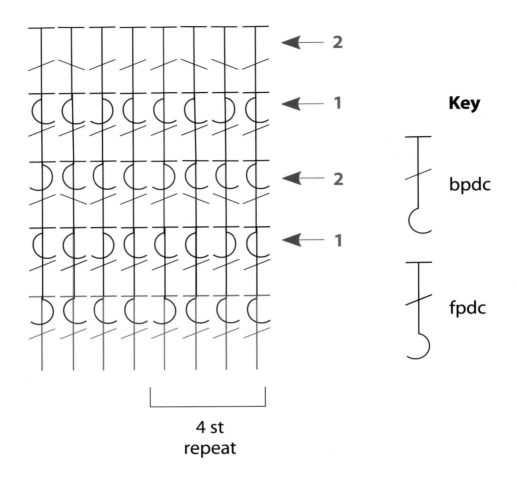

2

1

Key

2

1

bpdc

fpdc

4 st
repeat

Larger Size Only

Rnd 9: Ch 1, fpdc around same dc, [bpdc around each of next 3 dc, fpdc around next dc] 8 times, bpdc around each of next 10 dc, 2 bpdc around next dc, fpdc around next dc, 2 bpdc around next dc, bpdc around each of next 10 dc, [fpdc around next dc, bpdc around each of next 3 dc] 2 times, join with sl st around post of beg fpdc—2 sts inc'd, 66 sts.

Rnd 10: Ch 1, bpdc around same dc, bpdc around next dc, [fpdc around next dc, bpdc around each of next 3 dc] 8 times, fpdc around next dc, bpdc around each of next 21 dc, [fpdc around next dc, bpdc around each of next 3 dc] 2 times, fpdc around next dc, bpdc around last dc, join with sl st around post of beg bpdc.

Both Sizes

Separate Thumb

Next rnd: Ch 1, fpdc around same dc, [bpdc around each of next 3 dc, fpdc around next dc] 7 (8) times, bpdc around each of next 2 dc, [bpdc then fpdc around same dc], sk next 17 (19) sts, bpdc around each of next 3 dc, fpdc around next dc, bpdc around each of last 3 dc, join with sl st around post of beg fpdc—40 (48) dc, 17 (19) unworked sts for Thumb.

Upper Hand

Work Rnd 2 of Basketweave patt.
Work Rnds 1–2 of Basketweave patt 4 times.

Shape Top

Rnd 1: Ch 1, work Basketweave patt over 8 (10) sts, bpdc2tog, bpdc around next dc, place removable marker on bpdc just worked, bpdc2tog, work in patt over next 15 (19) sts, bpdc2tog, bpdc around next dc, place removable marker on bpdc just worked, bpdc2tog, work in patt over last 7 (9) sts, join with sl st to beg dc—4 sts dec'd, 36 (44) sts.

Note: Move markers up each rnd.

Rnd 2: Ch 1, work in est'd patt around, join with sl st to beg dc.

Rnd 3: Ch 1, [work in patt to 2 sts before marked st, bpdc2tog, bpdc around next dc, bpdc2tog] 2 times, work in patt to end—4 sts dec'd, 32 (40) sts.

Rnd 4: Ch 1, work in est'd patt around, join with sl st to beg dc.

Rnd 5: Ch 1, [work in patt to 2 sts before marked st, bpdc2tog, bpdc around next dc, bpdc2tog] 2 times, work in patt to end—4 sts dec'd, 28 (36) sts.

Rnd 6: Ch 1, [work in patt to 2 sts before marked st, bpdc2tog, bpdc around next dc, bpdc2tog] 2 times, work in patt to end—4 sts dec'd, 24 (32) sts.

Rnd 7: Ch 1, [work in patt to 2 sts before marked st, bpdc2tog, bpdc around next dc, bpdc2tog] 2 times, work in patt to end—4 sts dec'd, 20 (28) sts.

Larger Size Only

Rep Rnds 6–7—20 sts.

All Sizes

Next rnd: Ch 1, sc in blo of same dc, sc in blo of each dc around, join with sl st to top of beg sc. Fasten off, leaving 12"/30.5 cm tail. Turn Mitten inside out. Whipstitch last rnd of sc tog through blo of each sc. Draw taut, weave in tail.

Thumb

Join MC to center of Thumb gap leaving an 8"/20.5 cm tail.

Rnd 1: Ch 2 (counts as bpdc), bpdc around each of next 8 (9) dc, fpdc around next dc, bpdc around each of next 8 (9) dc, work 1 bpdc in gap, join with sl st around post of beg fpdc—19 (21) dc.

Rnd 2: Ch 1, bpdc2tog (same dc with next dc), bpdc around each of next 15 (17), bpdc2tog—17 (19) sts.

Rnd 3: Ch 1, bpdc around each of 1st 8 (9) dc, fpdc around next dc, bpdc around each of last 8 (9) dc, join with sl st around post of beg bpdc.

Rnd 4: Ch 1, bpdc around each dc, join with sl st around post of beg bpdc.

Rnds 5–6: Rep Rnds 3–4.

Rnd 7: Ch 1, bpdc in same dc, [bpdc2tog] 8 (9) times, join with sl st around post of beg bpdc—9 (10) sts.

Rnd 8: Ch 1, sc in blo of same dc, sc in blo of each dc around, join with sl st to top of beg sc.

Fasten off, leaving 10"/25.5 cm tail. Weave tail in and out of back lps of last rnd of sc. Draw taut, weave tail inside Mitten.

Left Mitten

Work as for Right Mitten to Thumb Gusset section.

Thumb Gusset

Rnd 1: Ch 1, fpdc around same dc, [bpdc around each of next 3 dc, fpdc around next dc] 1 (2) times, bpdc around each of next 2 dc, 2 bpdc around next dc, fpdc around next dc, 2 bpdc around next dc, bpdc around each of next 2 dc, [fpdc around next dc, bpdc around each of next 3 dc] 7 (8) times, join with sl st around post of beg fpdc—2 sts inc'd, 42 (50) sts.

Rnd 2: Ch 1, bpdc around same dc, bpdc around next dc, [fpdc around next dc, bpdc around each of next 3 dc] 1 (2) times, fpdc around next dc, [bpdc around next dc, 2 bpdc around next dc] 2 times, bpdc around next dc, [fpdc around next dc, bpdc around each of next 3 dc] 7

Overpass and Underpass mittens

(8) times, fpdc around next dc, bpdc around last dc, join with sl st around post of beg bpdc—2 sts inc'd, 44 (52) sts.

Rnd 3: Ch 1, fpdc around same dc, [bpdc around each of next 3 dc, fpdc around next dc] 1 (2) times, bpdc around each of next 4 dc, 2 bpdc around next dc, fpdc around next dc, 2 bpdc around next dc, bpdc around each of next 4 dc, [fpdc around next dc, bpdc around each of next 3 dc] 7 (8) times, join with sl st around post of beg fpdc—2 sts inc'd, 46 (54) sts.

Rnd 4: Ch 1, bpdc around same dc, bpdc around next dc, [fpdc around next dc, bpdc around each of next 3 dc] 1 (2) times, fpdc around next dc, bpdc around each of next 3 dc, 2 bpdc around next dc, bpdc around next dc, 2 bpdc around next dc, bpdc around each of next 3 dc, [fpdc around next dc, bpdc around each of next 3 dc] 7 (8) times, fpdc around next dc, bpdc around last dc, join with sl st around post of beg bpdc—2 sts inc'd, 48 (56) sts.

Rnd 5: Ch 1, fpdc around same dc, [bpdc around each of next 3 dc, fpdc around next dc] 1 (2) times, bpdc around each of next 6 dc, 2 bpdc around next dc, fpdc around next dc, 2 bpdc around next dc, bpdc around each of next 6 dc, [fpdc around next dc, bpdc around each of next 3 dc] 7 (8) times, join with sl st around post of beg fpdc—2 sts inc'd, 50 (58) sts.

Rnd 6: Ch 1, bpdc around same dc, bpdc around next dc, [fpdc around next dc, bpdc around each of next 3 dc] 1 (2) times, fpdc around next dc, bpdc around each of next 5 dc, 2 bpdc around next dc, bpdc around next dc, 2 bpdc around next dc, bpdc around each of next 5 dc, [fpdc around next dc, bpdc around each of next 3 dc] 7 (8) times, fpdc around next dc, bpdc around last dc, join with sl st around post of beg bpdc—2 sts inc'd, 52 (60) sts.

Rnd 7: Ch 1, fpdc around same dc, [bpdc around each of next 3 dc, fpdc around next dc] 1 (2) times, bpdc around each of next 8 dc, 2 bpdc around next dc, fpdc around next dc, 2 bpdc around next dc, bpdc around each of next 8 dc, [fpdc around next dc, bpdc around each of next 3 dc] 7 (8) times, join with sl st around post of beg fpdc—2 sts inc'd, 54 (62) sts.

Rnd 8: Ch 1, bpdc around same dc, bpdc around next dc, [fpdc around next dc, bpdc around each of next 3 dc] 1 (2) times, fpdc around next dc, bpdc around each of next 7 dc, 2 bpdc around next dc, bpdc around next dc, 2 bpdc around next dc, bpdc around each of next 7 dc, [fpdc around next dc, bpdc around each of next 3 dc] 7 (8) times, fpdc around next dc, bpdc around last dc, join with sl st around post of beg bpdc—2 sts inc'd, 56 (64) sts.

Larger Size Only

Rnd 9: Ch 1, fpdc around same dc, [bpdc around each of next 3 dc, fpdc around next dc] 2 times, bpdc around each of next 10 dc, 2 bpdc around next dc, fpdc around next dc, 2 bpdc around next dc, bpdc around each of next 10 dc, [fpdc around next dc, bpdc around each of next 3 dc] 8 times, join with sl st around post of beg fpdc—2 sts inc'd, 66 sts.

Rnd 10: Ch 1, bpdc around same dc, bpdc around next dc, [fpdc around next dc, bpdc around each of next 3 dc] 2 times, fpdc around next dc, bpdc around each of next 21 dc, bpdc, [fpdc around next dc, bpdc around each of next 3 dc] 8 times, fpdc around next dc, bpdc around last dc, join with sl st around post of beg bpdc.

Both Sizes

Separate Thumb

Next rnd: Ch 1, fpdc around same dc, [bpdc around each of next 3 dc, fpdc around next dc] 1 (2) times, bpdc around each of next 2 dc, [bpdc then fpdc around same dc], sk next 17 (19) sts, bpdc around each of next 3 dc, [fpdc around next dc, bpdc around each of next 3 dc] 7 (8) times, join with sl st around post of beg fpdc—40 (48) dc, 17 (19) unworked sts for Thumb.

Upper Hand

Work Rnd 2 of Basketweave patt.
Work Rnds 1–2 of Basketweave patt 4 times.

Shape Top and Thumb

Work as for Right Mitten.

Finishing

Attach CC to beg-ch edge of Cuff. With larger hook, loosely sl st in each ch around, fasten off. Weave in rem ends.

Frolic

Channel your inner child with these quirky mitts. The cuff will keep you interested with crossed stitches and eyelets. The hand uses a single crochet textured stitch to keep things simple and pretty. But choosing ribbons for the cuff is where the real fun lies! Go for a wide satin ribbon and your mitts will take on dramatic flair, or keep it simple with a narrow grosgrain ribbon.

FINISHED MEASUREMENTS
Hand circumference: 7^1/$_2$ (8^1/$_4$, 9^1/$_4$)"/19 (21, 23.5) cm
Length: 7^3/$_4$ (8, 8^1/$_2$)"/19.5 (20.5, 21.5) cm

SIZES
Women's Small (Medium, Large)
Shown in Small.

YARN
Premier Yarns Cotton Fair, fine weight #2 yarn (52% cotton, 48% acrylic; 317 yds/3.5 oz; 290 m/100 g)
• 1 skein #27-07 Bright Peach

HOOKS AND OTHER MATERIALS
• US C-2 (2.75 mm) crochet hook
• US D-3 (3.25 mm) crochet hook
• Tapestry needle
• 140"/356 cm of ^{5}/$_8$"/1.5 cm ribbon

GAUGE
26 sts x 24 rows in Pendulum patt = 4"/10 cm square using larger hook
Be sure to check your gauge!

STITCH PATTERN

Pendulum (even number of sts)

Rnd 1: Ch 1, sc in blo of same sc, sc in flo of next sc, [sc in blo of next sc, sc in flo of next sc] around, join with sl st to beg sc.

Rnd 2: Ch 1, sc in flo of same sc, sc in blo of next sc, [sc in flo of next sc, sc in blo of next sc] around; join with sl st to beg sc.

Rep Rnds 1–2 for patt.

Right Mitt

Cuff

With smaller hook, ch 48 (54, 60), join with sl st to beg ch to form ring, being careful not to twist ch.

Rnd 1: Ch 1, sc in same ch and each ch around, join with sl st to beg sc.

Rnd 2: Ch 1, fpdc in same sc and in each sc around, join with sl st to beg fpdc.

Rnd 3: Sl st in next 2 sts, sl st around post of same st where sl st was just worked (3rd st), ch 4 (counts as fptr + ch 1), fptr in first st of rnd, [sk next 4 sts, fptr in next st, ch 1, count 2 sts to right of fptr just made, fptr in this st] around, join with sl st to 3rd ch of beg ch-4—32 (36, 40) fptr, 16 (18, 20) ch-1 sps.

Rnd 4: Ch 1, fpdc in same tr, hdc in ch-1 sp, fpdc in next tr, [fpdc in next tr, hdc in ch-1 sp, fpdc in next tr] around, join with sl st to beg dc—32 (36, 40) fpdc, 16 (18, 20) hdc.

Rnd 5: Ch 1, fpdc in same dc, fpdc in each st around, join with sl st to beg fpdc.

Rnd 6: Ch 1, sc in blo of same st and in each st around, join with sl st to beg sc.

Rnd 7: Ch 3 (counts as dc), dc in next sc, ch 1, sk next sc, [dc in next 2 dc, ch 1, sk next sc] around, join with sl st to beg dc.

Rnd 8: Ch 1, sc in blo of same st and each st around, join with sl st to beg sc.

Rnds 9–15: Rep Rnds 2–8.

Hand

Switch to larger hook.

Work Rnds 1–2 of Pendulum patt 2 times.

Thumb Gusset

Rnd 1: Work in patt over 38 (42, 46) sts, ch 1, work in patt to end—1 st inc'd.

Rnd 2: Work in patt to ch-1 sp, [ch 1, 2 sc, ch 1] in ch-1 sp, work in patt to end—3 sts inc'd.

Rnd 3: Work in patt to ch-1 sp, ch 1, sc in sp, sc in blo of next sc, sc in flo of next sc, sc in next ch-1 sp, ch 1, work in patt to end—2 sts inc'd.

Rnd 4: Work in patt to ch-1 sp, ch 1, sc in sp, [sc in blo of next sc, sc in flo of next sc] 2 times, sc in next ch-1 sp, ch 1, work in patt to end—2 sts inc'd.

Rnd 5: Work in patt to ch-1 sp, ch 1, sc in sp, [sc in blo of next sc, sc in flo of next sc] 3 times, sc in next ch-1 sp, ch 1, work in patt to end—2 sts inc'd.

Rnd 6: Work in patt to ch-1 sp, ch 1, sc in sp, [sc in blo of next sc, sc in flo of next sc] 4 times, sc in next ch-1 sp, ch 1, work in patt to end—2 sts inc'd.

Rnd 7: Work in patt to ch-1 sp, ch 1, sc in sp, [sc in blo of next sc, sc in flo of next sc] 5 times, sc in next ch-1 sp, ch 1, work in patt to end—2 sts inc'd.

Rnd 8: Work in patt to ch-1 sp, ch 1, sc in sp, [sc in blo of next sc, sc in flo of next sc] 6 times, sc in next ch-1 sp, ch 1, work in patt to end—2 sts inc'd.

Rnd 9: Work in patt to ch-1 sp, ch 1, sk sp, [sc in blo of next sc, sc in flo of next sc] 7 times, sk next ch-1 sp, ch 1, work in patt to end.

Rnd 10: Work in patt to ch-1 sp, ch 1, sc in sp, [sc in flo of next sc, sc in blo of next sc] 7 times, sc in next ch-1 sp, ch 1, work in patt to end—2 sts inc'd.

Rnd 11: Work in patt to ch-1 sp, ch 1, sk sp, [sc in blo of next sc, sc in blo of next sc] 8 times, sk next ch-1 sp, ch 1, work in patt to end.

Rnd 12: Work in patt to ch-1 sp, ch 1, sc in sp, [sc in flo of next sc, sc in blo of next sc] 8 times, sc in next ch-1 sp, ch 1, work in patt to end—2 sts inc'd.

Medium & Large Sizes Only

Rnd 13: Work in patt to ch-1 sp, ch 1, sk sp, [sc in blo of next sc, sc in flo of next sc] 9 times, sk next ch-1 sp, ch 1, work in patt to end.

Rnd 14: Work in patt to ch-1 sp, ch 1, sc in sp, [sc in flo of next sc, sc in blo of next sc] 9 times, sc in next ch-1 sp, ch 1, work in patt to end—2 sts inc'd.

Large Size Only

Rnd 15: Work in patt to ch-1 sp, ch 1, sk sp, [sc in blo of next sc, sc in blo of next sc] 10 times, sk next ch-1 sp, ch 1, work in patt to end.

Rnd 16: Work in patt to ch-1 sp, ch 1, sc in sp, [sc in flo of next sc, sc in blo of next sc] 10 times, sc in next ch-1 sp, ch 1, work in patt to end—2 sts inc'd.

All Sizes

Next rnd: Work in patt to ch-1 sp, sc in sp, work in patt over next 18 (20, 22) sts, sc in next ch-1 sp, work in patt to end.

Next rnd: Work in patt over 38 (42, 46) sts, sk next 20 (22, 24) sc, work in patt over rem 10 (12, 14) sts—48 (54, 60) sc.

Upper Hand

Work Rnds 1–2 of Pendulum patt 4 times.

Next rnd: Ch 1, bpslst in same sc, bpslst in each sc around, fasten off.

Thumb

Attach yarn to center of Thumb gap. Beginning with Rnd 2 (1, 2) work 2 rnds of Pendulum patt.

Next rnd: Ch 1, bpslst in same sc, bpslst in each sc around, fasten off.

Left Mitt

Work as for Right Mitt to Thumb Gusset.

Thumb Gusset

Rnd 1: Work in patt over 10 (12, 14) sts, ch 1, work in patt to end—1 st inc'd.

Rnds 2–12 (14, 16): Work as for Right Mitt.

Next rnd: Work in patt to ch-1 sp, sc in sp, work in patt over next 18 (20, 22) sts, sc in next ch-1 sp, work in patt to end.

Next rnd: Work in patt over 10 (12, 14) sts, sk next 20 (22, 24) sc, work in patt over rem 38 (42, 46) sts—48 (54, 60) sc.

Complete remainder of Left Mitt as for Right Mitt.

Finishing

Weave in ends. Cut ribbon into four 35"/89 cm lengths. Weave ribbon in and out of eyelets from Rnds 7 and 13 of Cuff. Loosely tie ribbon. Try on mitts to make sure they will fit over your hands since the ribbon will be inelastic. Tie ribbons in a bow.

> **TIP:** Keep track of where you are in the Pendulum stitch pattern by reading your work. Always work into the front/back loop of the next stitch in the opposite way of what was worked the previous round. Look at the base of the single crochet you're about to work into. If you can see a little line across the base of the stitch, that means it was worked through the back loop of its previous stitch; work through the *front* loop of this stitch. If you can see the entire front legs of the stitch, that means it was worked through the front loop of its previous stitch; work through the *back* loop of this stitch.

ooking for an everyday pair of fingerless mitts? Here they are! Reverse single crochet and a folded cuff give these mitts a finished look, while a simple stitch pattern keeps them unfancy and ultra-wearable. These would work great for guys, too. Wear Plain Jane on their own, or use as a base for Holey Color! Both pairs are designed to fit perfectly with one another.

FINISHED MEASUREMENTS
Palm circumference: 7 ($7^3/_4$, $8^1/_2$, $9^1/_4$)"/18 (19.5, 21.5, 23.5) cm
Cuff: 6 ($6^1/_2$, 7, $7^1/_2$)"/15 (16.5, 18, 19) cm
Length: $9^1/_4$ ($9^1/_4$, 10, 10)"/23.5 (23.5, 25.5, 25.5) cm

SIZES
Women's Small (Medium, Large, Extra Large)
Shown in Small.

YARN
Deborah Norville Collection Serenity Sock Solids by Premier Yarns, super fine weight #1 yarn (50% superwash merino wool, 25% bamboo, 25% nylon; 230 yds/1.75 oz; 210 m/50 g)
• 1 skein #DN150-11 Charcoal

HOOKS AND OTHER MATERIALS
- US C-2 (2.75 mm) crochet hook
- US B-1 (2.25 mm) crochet hook
- Tapestry needle

GAUGE
34 sts x 26 rows in Linen St patt = 4"/10 cm square using larger hook

28 sts x 18 rows in Offset DC patt = 4"/10 cm square using smaller hook

Be sure to check your gauge!

STITCH PATTERNS
Linen Stitch (even number of sts)
Row 1 (WS): Ch 1, sc in same st, ch 1, sk next st, [sc in next st, ch 1, sk next st] across, join with sl st to beg sc, turn.

Row 2 (RS): Ch 1, [sc in next ch-1 sp, ch 1, sk next sc] across, join with sl st to beg sc, turn.

Rep Row 2 for patt.

Offset DC (any number of sts)
Row 1: Sl st in sp between next 2 dc, ch 3 (counts as dc), [dc in sp between next 2 dc] across, join with sl st to beg dc, turn.

Rep Row 1 for patt.

Right Mitt

With larger hook, ch 52 (56, 60, 64), join with sl st to beg ch.

Cuff
Note: Cuff is worked in joined rows.

Set-up row (RS): Ch 1, sc in same sp, sc in each ch across, join with sl st to beg sc, turn—52 (56, 60, 64) sc.

Row 1 (WS): Work Row 1 of Linen St patt across—26 (28, 30, 32) sc, 26 (28, 30, 32) ch-1 sps.

Row 2: Work Row 2 of Linen St patt across.

Rows 3–10: Rep Row 2 of Linen St patt 8 more times.

Fold Cuff in half, bringing beg-ch edge up and even with Row 10, so wrong sides of Cuff are facing. Switch to smaller hook.

Row 11 (Joining Row): Ch 1, sc2tog (next ch-1 sp from Row 10 tog with 1st ch from beg-ch edge), [sc2tog (next st from Row 10 tog with next ch from beg-ch edge)] across, join with sl st to beg sc, turn.

Arm
Small Size Only
Row 1 (WS): Ch 3 (counts as dc), dc in next sc, dc2tog, dc in next 4 sc, [dc2tog, dc in next 3 sc] 7 times, dc2tog, dc in next 4 sc, dc2tog, dc in last sc, turn—10 sts dec'd, 42 sts.

Medium Size Only
Row 1 (WS): Ch 3 (counts as dc), dc in next 2 sc, dc2tog, [dc in next 3 dc, dc2tog] 9 times, dc in last 6 dc, turn—10 sts dec'd, 46 sts.

Large Size Only
Row 1 (WS): Ch 3 (counts as dc), dc in next 3 sc, dc2tog, [dc in next 4 dc, dc2tog] 9 times, turn—10 sts dec'd, 50 sts.

Extra Large Size Only
Row 1 (WS): Ch 3 (counts as dc), dc in next 3 sc, dc2tog, [dc in next 4 dc, dc2tog] 9 times, dc in last 4 dc, turn—10 sts dec'd, 54 sts.

All Sizes
Note: When working Row 2, be sure not to work a dc between the dc2tog from Row 1.

Row 2 (RS): Work Row 1 of Offset DC patt to end.

Rows 3–14: Cont in patt.

Thumb Opening
Row 1 (WS): Ch 3 (counts as dc), dc in sp between next 2 dc, [dc in sp between next 2 dc across], end dc in same st as beg ch-3, do not join, turn—43 (47, 51, 55) dc.

Row 2 (RS): Ch 3 (counts as dc), sk sp between next 2 dc, sk next dc, [dc in sp between next 2 dc] across to last 2 dc, sk next dc, dc in last dc, turn—42 (46, 50, 54) dc.

Rows 3–9 (9, 11, 11): [Rep Rows 1–2] 3 (3, 3, 3) times, then rep Row 1.

Upper Hand
Row 1 (RS): Ch 3, sk sp between next 2 dc, sk next dc, [dc in sp between next 2 dc] across to last 2 dc, sk next dc, dc in last dc, join with sl st to beg dc, turn—42 (46, 50, 54) dc.

Rows 2–11: Work in Offset DC patt to end. Do not turn at the end of Row 11.

Row 12: Ch 1, working from left to right, sc in next sp, [sc in next sp] across. Fasten off.

Left Mitt

Work as for Right Mitt.

Finishing

Thumb Edging
Using smaller hook, attach yarn with sl st to lower Thumb opening.

Rnd 1 (RS): Ch 1, Work 32 (32, 36, 36) sc evenly around opening, join with sl st to beg sc.

Rnd 2: Ch 1, working from left to right, sc in next sp, [sc in next sc] around, join with sl st to beg sc. Fasten off.

Weave in ends.

Holey Color!

Self-striping and variegated sock yarns are a perfect match for the open pattern in this pair of mitts. The big holes serve a dual duty. Worn alone, these mitts work great in transitional weather where not too much extra warmth is needed. Layered over Plain Jane, you can still have the same fun holey look but with more coverage to protect your hands from the elements.

FINISHED MEASUREMENTS
Palm circumference: $6^{1}/_{2}$ ($7^{1}/_{4}$, 8, $8^{3}/_{4}$)"/16.5 (18.5, 20.5, 22) cm
Note: Worked in Wool-Free Sock, this mitt is very stretchy. If you are between sizes, go down a size.
Length: $7^{3}/_{4}$ ($7^{3}/_{4}$, $8^{1}/_{2}$, $8^{1}/_{2}$)"/19.5 (19.5, 21.5, 21.5) cm

SIZES
Women's Extra Small/Small (Small/Medium, Medium/Large, Large/Extra Large)
Shown in Extra Small/Small.

YARN

Premier Yarns Wool-Free Sock, super fine weight #1 yarn
(93% acrylic, 7% PBT; 235 yds/1.75 oz; 215 m/50 g)
• 1 (2, 2, 2) skein(s) #08 Vegas Lights

HOOK AND OTHER MATERIALS

• US B-1 (2.25 mm) crochet hook
• Tapestry needle

GAUGE

30 sts x 11 rows in Holey Color! patt = 4"/10 cm square
Be sure to check your gauge!

NOTES

• This mitt is worked sideways and seamed.

STITCH PATTERN

Holey Color!
***(begins with a multiple of 5 sts + 2; st count is increased
on Rows 1 and 3 and is returned to the original count
on Rows 2 and 4)***
Row 1 (RS): Ch 3 (counts as dc), sk next dc, [6 dc in next ch-
3 sp] across, dc in last dc, turn.
Row 2 (WS): Ch 4 (counts as dc + ch 1), sk next 2 dc, [dc in
next 2 dc, ch 3, sk next 4 dc] across, ch 1, sk last 2 dc, dc
in last dc, turn.
Row 3: Ch 3 (counts as dc), 3 dc in next ch-1 sp, [6 dc in next
ch-3 sp] across, 3 dc in next ch-1 sp, dc in last dc, turn.
Row 4: Ch 3 (counts as dc), dc in next dc, [ch 3, sk next 4 dc,
dc in next 2 dc] across, turn.
Rep Rows 1–4 for patt.

Holey Color!

Key

○   ch

┬   dc

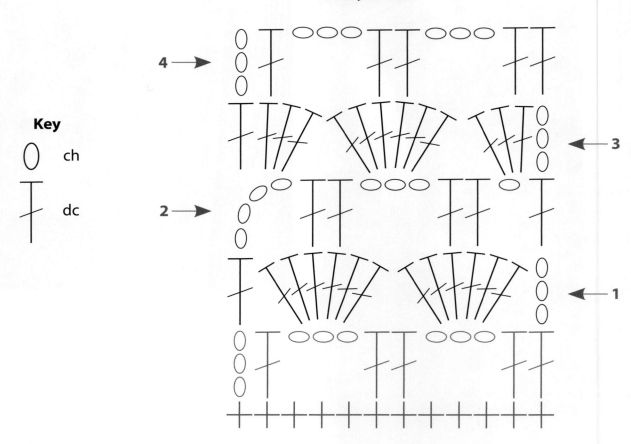

Right Mitt

Ch 53 (53, 58, 58).

Set-up row 1 (RS): Sc in 2nd ch from hook and each ch across, turn—52 (52, 57, 57) sc.

Set-up row 2 (WS): Ch 3 (counts as dc), dc in next sc, [ch 3, sk next 3 sc, dc in next 2 sc] across, turn.

Work Rows 1–4 of Holey Color! patt 4 (4, 5, 5) times, then [rep Row 1] 1 (0, 1, 0) more time.

Next row (WS): Ch 1, sc in 1st dc, [sc in next sc, sc2tog, sc in next 2 sc] across, end sc in last dc. Do not fasten off.

Upper Edging

Turn work 90 degrees.

Row 1 (WS): Ch 1, work sc evenly along side of work at a rate of 2.5 sc for every row, taking care that you end up with an odd number of sc, turn.

Row 2 (RS): Ch 1, sc in blo of each sc across, turn.

Row 3 (WS): Ch 1, sl st in same sc, [dc in next sc, sl st in next sc] across. Do not fasten off.

Join Sides of Mitt

Fold up mitt so that the last row of main mitt section worked and the beg-ch edges are tog with RS facing each other, and WS facing you.

Row 1: Sl st sides of Upper Edging tog; sl st tog each of 1st 12 (12, 14, 14) sts from side of main mitt; working along beg-ch edge only, sc in next 18 (20, 22, 24) chs; working through both edges again, sk 18 (20, 22, 24) sts along final mitt row, sl st tog rem 22 (20, 22, 20) sts, do not fasten off. Turn mitt RS out.

Lower Edging

Note: The Lower Edging is worked in joined rows.

Row 1 (WS): Ch 1, work sc evenly along side of work at a rate of 2.5 sc for every row, taking care that you end up with an odd number of sc, join with sl st to beg sc, turn.

Row 2 (RS): Ch 1, sc in blo of each sc across, join with sl st to beg sc, turn.

Row 3 (WS): Ch 1, sl st in same sc, dc in next sc, [sl st in next sc, dc in next sc] across, join with sl st to beg sl st. Fasten off.

Thumbhole Edging

Attach yarn to lower Thumb gap with sl st.

Row 1 (RS): Ch 1, sc in blo of each sc across, join with sl st to beg sc, turn.

Row 2 (WS): Ch 1, [sl st in next sc, dc in next sc] across, join with sl st to beg sc. Fasten off.

Holey Color! worn over a pair of Plain Janes

Left Mitt

Work as for Right Mitt.

Finishing

Weave in ends.

Radiate

Why limit yourself? Instead of standard top-to-bottom or side-to-side construction, these mitts begin from the thumb and work their way out. This is a great chance to show off shading and striping yarns. Or do a little stash-busting and stripe your scraps!

FINISHED MEASUREMENTS
Palm Circumference: 6^1/$_2$ (7^1/$_2$, 8^1/$_2$)"/16.5 (19, 21.5) cm
Length: 6^1/$_2$"/16.5 cm

SIZES
Women's Small (Medium, Large)
Shown in Small.

YARN
Wisdom Yarns Poems Sock, super fine weight #1 yarn (75% superwash wool, 25% nylon; 459 yds/3.5 oz; 420 m/100 g)
• 1 ball #966 Pulsar

HOOK AND OTHER MATERIALS
• US B-1 (2.25 mm) crochet hook
• Tapestry needle

GAUGE
26 sts x 32 rows in sc = 4"/10 cm square
Be sure to check your gauge!

NOTES
• This mitt is constructed from the thumb outward. After the thumb is made, work continues in joined rows as circular increases are made. After the circle shape is finished, the top of the hand is worked back and forth over about half the stitches. Then the yarn is rejoined to the unworked stitches from the other half of the circle and the palm of the hand is worked.
• This pattern only requires one ball of the specified yarn to complete. However, if you are using a self-shading or striping yarn (as shown), you may want to purchase two balls. This will give you more freedom in picking and choosing colors from the ball.
• To achieve a matching pair: Begin the thumb for each hand at the same point in the color sequence. When reattaching the yarn at the palm section, begin at the same point in the color sequence for the palm as you did for the top of the hand.

STITCH GUIDE
Spike Stitch
Insert hook in st indicated, pull up a lp even with current row, yo and pull through both lps on hook.

Right Mitt

Note: Mitt is worked in joined rows.

Thumb

Ch 20 (22, 24), join with sl st through blo to form ring.

Row 1 (RS): Ch 1, sc in same st, sc through blo of each ch around, join with sl st to beg sc, turn—20 (22, 24) sc.

Row 2 (WS): Ch 1, sc in each sc around, join with sl st to beg sc, turn.

Rows 3–6: Rep Row 2.

Small Size Only

Row 7: Ch 1, [sc in next 4 sc, 2 sc in next sc] 4 times, join with sl st to beg sc, turn—24 sc.

Medium Size Only

Row 7: Ch 1, [sc in next 10 sc, 2 sc in next sc] 2 times, join with sl st to beg sc, turn—24 sc.

Large Size only

Row 7: Rep Row 2.

All Sizes

Row 8: Rep Row 2.

Increase for Hand

Row 1 (RS): Ch 1, [sc in next 3 sc, 2 sc in next sc] 6 times, join with sl st to beg sc, turn—6 sts inc'd, 30 sc.

Row 2 (WS): Ch 1, sc in next 2 sc, [2 sc in next sc, sc in next 4 sc] 5 times, 2 sc in next sc, sc in last 2 sc, join with sl st to beg sc, turn—6 sts inc'd, 36 sc.

Row 3: Ch 1, [sc in next 5 sc, 2 sc in next sc] 6 times, join with sl st to beg sc, turn—6 sts inc'd, 42 sc.

Row 4: Ch 1, sc in next 3 sc, [spike st in sc from 3 rows below, sc in next 7 sc] 5 times, spike st in sc from 3 rows below, sc in last 4 sc, join with sl st to beg sc, turn—6 sts inc'd, 48 sts.

Row 5: Ch 1, [sc in next 7 sts, 2 sc in next sc] 6 times, join with sl st to beg sc, turn—6 sts inc'd, 54 sc.

Row 6: Ch 1, [sc in next 9 sc, spike st in sc from 3 rows below] 6 times, join with sl st to beg sc, turn—6 sts inc'd, 60 sts.

Row 7: Ch 1, sc in each sc across, join with sl st to beg sc, turn.

Row 8: Ch 1, sc in next 5 sc, [spike st in sc from 3 rows below, sc in next 10 sc] 5 times, spike st in sc from 3 rows below, sc in last 5 sc, join with sl st to beg sc, turn—6 sts inc'd, 66 sc.

Row 9: Sl st in 1st sc, ch 3 (counts as dc), dc in blo of each st across, join with sl st to top of beg ch-3, turn.

Rows 10–11: Ch 1, sc in each sc across, join with sl st to beg sc, turn.

Row 12: Ch 1, sc in next 5 sc, [2 sc in next sc, sc in next 10 sc] 5 times, 2 sc in next sc, sc in last 5 sc, join with sl st to beg sc, turn—6 sts inc'd, 72 sc.

Row 13: Ch 1, 2 sc in next sc, sc in each sc to last sc, 2 sc in last sc, join with sl st to beg sc, turn—2 sts inc'd, 74 sc.

Row 14: Ch 1, sc in next 13 sc, [spike st in sc from 3 rows below, sc in next 12 sc] 4 times, spike st in sc from 3 rows below, sc in last 13 sc, spike st in sc from 3 rows below, join with sl st to beg sc, turn—6 sts inc'd, 80 sts.

Row 15: Ch 1, 2 sc in next st, sc in each sc to last sc, 2 sc in last sc, join with sl st to beg sc, turn—2 sts inc'd, 82 sc.

Row 16: Ch 1, sc in next 8 sc, [spike st in sc from 3 rows below, sc in next 13 sc] 5 times, spike st in sc from 3 rows below, sc in last 9 sc, join with sl st to beg sc, turn—6 sts inc'd, 88 sts.

Row 17: Ch 1, 2 sc in next st, sc in each sc to last sc, 2 sc in last sc, join with sl st to beg sc, turn—2 sts inc'd, 90 sc.

Row 18: Ch 1, sc in next 17 sc, [spike st in sc from 3 rows below, sc in next 14 sc] 4 times, spike st in sc from 3 rows below, sc in last 17 sc, spike st in sc from 3 rows below, join with sl st to beg sc, turn—6 sts inc'd, 96 sts.

Back of Hand

Note: Decreases are made at the beginning and end of each row by skipping a stitch. Two increases are worked into each row to compensate, making the stitch count the same for each row.

Row 1 (RS): Sl st in 1st 2 sts, ch 3 (counts as dc), dc in blo of next 44 sts, turn—45 dc.

Row 2 (WS): Sk 1st dc, sc in next 13 dc, 2 sc in next dc, sc in next 15 dc, 2 sc in next dc, sc in next 12 dc, sk next dc, sc in top of last dc, turn.

Row 3: Sk 1st sc, sc in next 18 sc, 2 sc in next sc, sc in next 5 sc, 2 sc in next sc, sc in next 17 sc, sk next sc, sc in last sc, turn.

Row 4: Sk 1st sc, sc in next 7 sc, 2 sc in next sc, sc in next 27 sc, 2 sc in next sc, sc in next 6 sc, sk next sc, sc in last sc, turn.

Row 5: Sk 1st sc, sc in next 13 sc, 2 sc in next sc, sc in next 15 sc, 2 sc in next sc, sc in next 12 sc, sk next sc, sc in last sc, turn.

Row 6: Sk 1st sc, sc in next 2 sc, spike st in sc from 3 rows below, sc in next 19 sc, spike st in sc from 3 rows below, sk sc behind spike st just made, sc in next 19 sc, spike st in sc from 3 rows below, sc in next sc, sk next sc, sc in last sc, turn.

Row 7: Sk 1st sc, sl st in next sc, ch 3 (counts as dc), dc in next 4 sc, hdc in next 7 sc, sc in next 2 sc, 2 sc in next sc, sc in next 13 sc, 2 sc in next sc, sc in next 2 sc, hdc in next 7 sc, dc in next 4 sc, sk next sc, dc in last sc, turn.

Row 8: Sk 1st dc, sc in next 12 sts, spike st in sc from 3 rows below, sc in next 19 sts, spike st in sc from 3 rows below, sc in next 11 sts, sk next dc, sc in last dc, turn.

Row 9: Sk 1st sc, sc in next 14 sc, 2 sc in next sc, sc in next 13 sc, 2 sc in next sc, sc in next 2 sc, hdc in next 7 sc, dc in next 4 sc, sk next sc, dc in last sc, turn.

Row 10: Sk 1st dc, sc in next 2 scs, spike st in sc from 2 rows below, sc in next 19 sts, spike st in sc from 3 rows below, sk sc behind spike st just made, sc in next 19 sts, spike st in sc from 2 rows below, sc in next sc, sk next sc, sc in last sc, turn.

Row 11: Rep Row 7.

Medium & Large Sizes Only

Row 12: Sk 1st sc, sc in next 7 sc, 2 sc in next sc, sc in next 27 sc, 2 sc in next sc, sc in next 6 sc, sk next sc, sc in last sc, turn.

Row 13: Sk 1st st, sl st in next sc, ch 3 (counts as dc), dc in blo of next 12 sc, 2 dc in blo of next sc, dc in blo of next 15 sc, 2 dc in blo of next sc, dc in blo of next 12 sc, sk next sc, dc in last sc, turn.

Large Size Only

Rows 14–15: Rep Rows 12–13.

All Sizes

Next row (WS): Sk 1st sc, sc in each of next 18 sts, 2 sc in next st, sc in each of next 5 sts, 2 sc in next st, sc in each of next 17 sts, sk next st, sc in last st, turn.

Next row (RS): Sk 1st sc, sl st in next sc, ch 3 (counts as dc), dc in blo of each sc to last 2 sc, sk next sc, dc in last sc. Fasten off.

Palm

With RS facing, sk 3 sts counterclockwise from Row 1 of Back of Hand, join yarn with sl st.

Row 1 (RS): Ch 3 (counts as dc), dc in blo of next 44 sts, turn.

Rows 2–8: Work as for Back of Hand.

Row 9: Sk 1st sc, sl st in next sc, ch 3 (counts as dc), dc in next 4 sc, hdc in next 7 sc, sc in next 2 sc, 2 sc in next sc, sc in next 13 sc, 2 sc in next sc, sc in next 13 sc, sk next sc, sc in last sc, turn.

Rows 10–11: Work as for Back of Hand.

Medium & Large Sizes Only

Row 12: Sk 1st sc, sc in next 7 sc, 2 sc in next sc, sc in next 27 sc, 2 sc in next sc, sc in next 6 sc, sk next sc, sc in last sc, turn.

Row 13: Sk 1st st, sl st in next sc, ch 3 (counts as dc), dc in blo of next 12 sc, 2 dc in blo of next sc, dc in blo of next 15 sc, 2 dc in blo of next sc, dc in blo of next 12 sc, sk next sc, dc in last sc, turn.

Large Size Only

Rows 14–15: Rep Rows 12–13.

All Sizes

Next row (WS): Sk 1st sc, sc in next 18 sts, 2 sc in next st, sc in next 5 sts, 2 sc in next st, sc in next 17 sts, sk next st, sc in last st, turn.

Next row (RS): Sk 1st sc, sl st in next sc, ch 3 (counts as dc), dc in blo of each sc to last 2 sc, sk next sc, dc in last sc. Fasten off, leaving 18"/45.5 cm. Join last row of Palm to last row of Back of Hand using mattress stitch, loosely, working through blo of each st.

Top Edging

Join yarn to top of mitt at seam.

Rnd 1: Work 50 (58, 66) sl sts evenly and loosely around edge.

Rnd 2: Ch 1, hdc in blo of 1st sl st and each sl st around, join with sl st to top of beg hdc.

Rnd 3: Ch 1, fpdc in 1st hdc and each hdc around, join with sl st to beg fpdc.

Rnd 4: Ch 1, work rev sc evenly around. Fasten off.

Cuff

Join yarn to bottom of mitt at seam.

Rnd 1: Work 42 (50, 58) sl sts evenly and loosely around edge.

Rnd 2: Ch 1, hdc in blo of 1st sl st and each sl st around, join with sl st to top of beg hdc.

Rnd 3: Ch 1, fpdc in 1st hdc and each hdc around, join with sl st to beg fpdc.

Rnds 4–6: Ch 1, fpdc in 1st fpdc and each fpdc around, join with sl st to beg fpdc.

Fasten off.

Left Mitt

Work as for Right Mitt to Back of Hand.

Back of Hand

With RS facing, sk next 49 sc, attach yarn with sl st in next sc.

Row 1 (RS): Ch 3 (counts as dc), dc in blo of next 44 sts, turn—45 dc.

Rows 2–8: Work as for Right Mitt.

Row 9: Sk 1st sc, sl st in next sc, ch 3 (counts as dc), dc in next 4 sc, hdc in next 7 sc, sc in next 2 sc, 2 sc in next sc, sc in next 13 sc, 2 sc in next sc, sc in next 13 sc, sk next sc, sc in last sc, turn.

Complete remainder of Back of Hand as for Right Mitt.

Palm

With RS facing, sk 3 sts counterclockwise from Row 1 of Back of Hand, join yarn with sl st.

Row 1 (RS): Ch 3 (counts as dc), dc in blo of next 44 sts, turn.

Rows 2–8: Work as for Back of Hand.

Row 9: Sk 1st fpsc, sc in next 14 sc, 2 sc in next sc, sc in next 13 sc, 2 sc in next sc, sc in next 2 sc, hdc in next 7 sc, dc in next 4 sc, sk next sc, dc in last sc, turn.

Complete remainder of Palm as for Right Mitt.

Top Edging, Cuff

Work as for Right Mitt.

Finishing

Weave in ends.

Bounty
Mitts

Bobbles—you either love 'em or hate 'em. For all you bobble lovers out there, these are the mitts for you. Worked from the cuff up, Bounty Mitts incorporate cables, ribbing, and plenty of bobbles. As shown, made in a yarn comprised of luxurious fibers, this project is a special treat for your hands.

FINISHED MEASUREMENTS
Hand circumference: 7^1/$_2$ (8^1/$_2$, 9^1/$_2$)"/19 (21.5, 24) cm
Length: 6^1/$_2$ (7^1/$_2$, 8)"/16.5 (19, 20.5) cm

SIZES
Women's Small (Medium, Large)
Shown in Small.

YARN
Fibra Natura Llamalini, medium weight #4 yarn (40% royal llama, 35% silk bourette, 25% linen; 109 yds/1.75 oz; 100 m/ 50 g)
• 2 skeins #106 Lotus

HOOK AND OTHER MATERIALS
• US G-6 (4.0 mm) crochet hook
• Tapestry needle

GAUGE
15 sts x 18 rows in sc = 4"/10 cm square
Be sure to check your gauge!

NOTES
• The cuff is worked in the round.
• The hand is worked back and forth in joined rows.

STITCH GUIDE
Extended Single Crochet (esc)
Insert hook into st indicated and pull up a lp (2 lps on hook), ch 1, yo, and pull through both lps on hook.

Bobble (B)

Yo, insert hook in next sc, yo, and pull up a lp (3 lps on hook), yo, pull through 2 lps, [yo, insert hook in same sc, yo, pull up a lp, yo, and pull through 2 lps] 2 times, yo, pull through all 4 lps, insert hook from back to front through same sc, sl st.

Crab Stitch

Working from *left* to right, sc in each st around, as follows: With RS facing, insert the hook, from front to back, in the next st to the right. Yo, pull up a lp, yo, pull through 2 lps. Repeat around.

STITCH PATTERN

Right Hand Cable (worked over 10 sts)

Row 1 (RS): Sc in next 2 sc, sk next 3 dc from previous row, [fpdc around post of next dc] 3 times, working in front of fpdcs just made, fpdc around post of first skipped dc, [fpdc around post of next dc] 2 times, sc in next 2 sc.

Row 2 and all WS rows: Sc in each st across.

Row 3: Sc in next 2 sc, [fpdc around post of next dc from 2 rows below] 6 times, sk 6 sc behind fpdcs just worked, sc in next 2 sc.

Row 5: [Fpdc around post of next dc from 2 rows below] 3 times, sk 3 sts behind fpdcs just made, sc in next 4 sc, [fpdc around post of next dc] 3 times.

Row 7: [Fpdc around post of next dc from 2 rows below] 3 times, sc in next sc, [B in next sc] 2 times, sc in next sc, [fpdc around post of next dc from 2 rows below] 3 times.

Rows 9, 11, 13, and 15: Rep Row 7.

Row 17: Sc in next 2 sc, [fpdc around post of next dc from 2 rows below] 6 times, sk 6 sc behind fpdcs just worked, sc in next 2 sc.

Row 19: Sc in first 3 sc, fpdc2tog around 3rd and 4th dc, fpdc2tog around 2nd and 5th dc, fpdc2tog around 1st and 6th dc, sk 4 sc behind fpdcs just made, sc in next 3 sc—9 sts.

Row 20: Sc in each st across.

Left Hand Cable (worked over 10 sts)

Row 1 (RS): Sc in next 2 sc, sk next 3 dc from previous row, [fpdc around post of next dc] 3 times, working behind fpdcs just made, fpdc around post of 1st skipped dc, [fpdc around post of next dc] 2 times, sc in next 2 sc.

Rows 2–20: Work as for Right Hand Cable.

Right Mitt

Ch 27 (31, 35). Join with sl st to bump of 1st ch to form ring, being careful not to twist chs.

Cuff

Rnd 1: Ch 1, working through bump of each ch, esc in same ch, esc in each ch around, join with sl st to form ring—27 (31, 35) esc.

Rnd 2: Ch 1, esc in same st, [fpdc in next st, esc in next st] 5 (6, 7) times, fpdc in next 6 sts, [esc in next st, fpdc in next st] 5 (6, 7) times, join with sl st to beg esc.

Rnds 3–6: Rep Rnd 2.

Hand

Begin working in joined rows.

Rnd 1: Ch 1, sc in next 9 (11, 13) sts, work Row 1 of Right Hand Cable patt over 10 sts, sc in each sc to last st, 2 sc in last sc, join with sl st to beg sc, turn—29 (33, 37) sts.

Rnd 2 (WS): Ch 1, sc in each st around, join with sl st to beg sc, turn.

Thumb Gusset

Rnd 1 (Inc): Ch 1, sc in next 9 (11, 13) sc, work Row 3 of Right Hand Cable patt over 10 sts, sc in next 3 (4, 5) sc, 2 sc in next sc, sc in next sc, 2 sc in next sc, sc in last 4 (5, 6) sc, join with sl st to beg sc, turn—2 sts inc'd.

Rnd 2 (WS): Ch 1, sc in each st around, join with sl st to beg sc, turn—31 (35, 39) sc.

Rnd 3 (Inc): Ch 1, sc in next 9 (11, 13) sc, work Row 5 of Right Hand Cable patt over 10 sts, sc in next 3 (4, 5) sc, 2 sc in next sc, sc in next 3 sc, 2 sc in next sc, sc in last 4 (5, 6) sc, join with sl st to beg sc, turn—2 sts inc'd.

Rnd 4: Ch 1, sc in each st around, join with sl st to beg sc, turn—33 (37, 41) sc.

Rnd 5 (Inc): Ch 1, sc in next 9 (11, 13) sc, work Row 7 of Right Hand Cable over 10 sts, sc in next 3 (4, 5) sc, 2 sc in next sc, sc in next 5 sc, 2 sc in next sc, sc in last 4 (5, 6) sc, join with sl st to beg sc, turn—2 sts inc'd.

Rnd 6: Ch 1, sc in each st around, join with sl st to beg sc, turn—35 (39, 43) sc.

Rnd 7 (Inc): Ch 1, sc in next 9 (11, 13) sc, work Row 9 of Right Hand Cable patt over 10 sts, sc in next 3 (4, 5) sc, 2 sc in next sc, sc in next 7 sc, 2 sc in next sc, sc in last 4 (5, 6) sc, join with sl st to beg sc, turn—2 sts inc'd.

Rnd 8: Ch 1, sc in each st around, join with sl st to beg sc, turn—37 (41, 45) sc.

Rnd 9 (Inc): Ch 1, sc in next 9 (11, 13) sc, work Row 11 of Right Hand Cable patt over 10 sts, sc in next 3 (4, 5) sc, 2 sc in next sc, sc in next 9 sc, 2 sc in next sc, sc in last 4 (5, 6) sc, join with sl st to beg sc, turn—2 sts inc'd.

Rnd 10: Ch 1, sc in each st around, join with sl st to beg sc, turn—39 (43, 47) sc.

Small Size Only

Rnd 11: Ch 1, sc in next 9 sc, work Row 13 of Right Hand Cable patt over 10 sts, sc in last 20 sc, join with sl st to beg sc, turn—39 sc.

Rnd 12: Ch 1, sc in each st around, join with sl st to beg sc, turn—39 sc.

Rnd 13: Ch 1, sc in next 9 sc, work Row 15 of Right Hand Cable patt over 10 sts, sc in next 4 sc, sk next 10 sc, ch 1, sc in last 5 sc, join with sl st to beg sc, turn—29 sts.

Rnd 14: Ch 1, sc in each st around, join with sl st to beg sc, turn.

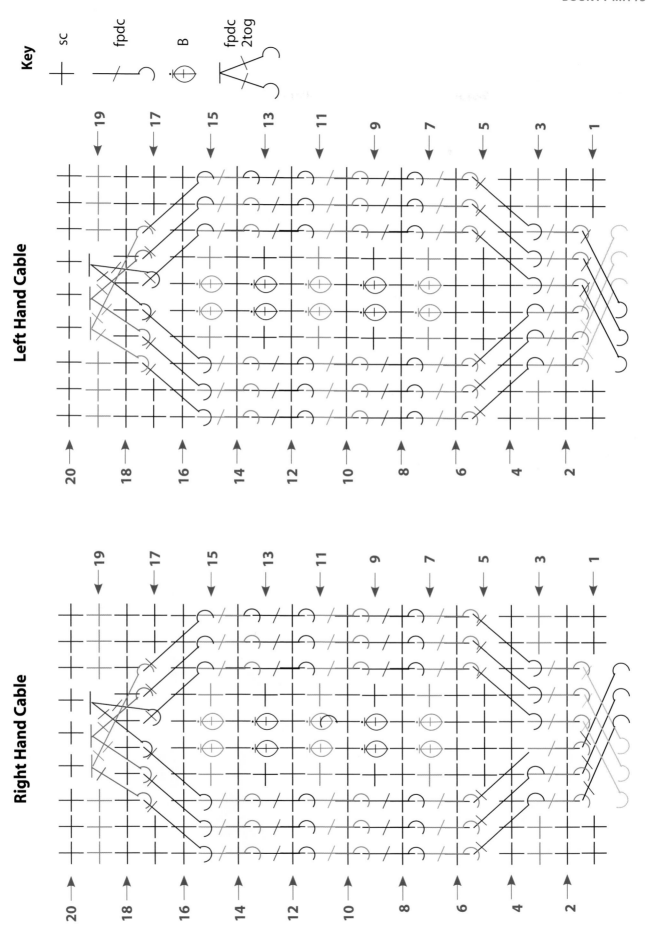

Key
sc
fpdc
B
fpdc
2tog

Left Hand Cable

Right Hand Cable

Medium Size Only

Rnd 11 (Inc): Ch 1, sc in next 11 sc, work Row 13 of Right Hand Cable patt over 10 sts, sc in next 4 sc, 2 sc in next sc, sc in next 11 sc, 2 sc in next sc, sc in last 5 sc, join with sl st to beg sc, turn—2 sts inc'd.

Rnd 12: Ch 1, sc in each st around, join with sl st to beg sc, turn—45 sc.

Rnd 13: Ch 1, sc in next 11 sc, work Row 15 of Right Hand Cable patt over 10 sts, sc in last 24 sc, join with sl st to beg sc, turn.

Rnd 14: Ch 1, sc in each st around, join with sl st to beg sc, turn.

Rnd 15: Ch 1, sc in next 11 sc, work Row 15 of Right Hand Cable patt (for a second time) over 10 sts, sc in next 5 sc, sk next 12 sc, ch 1, sc in last 6 sc, join with sl st to beg sc, turn—33 sts.

Rnd 16: Ch 1, sc in each st around, join with sl st to beg sc, turn.

Large Size Only

Rnd 11: Ch 1, sc in next 13 sc, work Row 13 of Right Hand Cable patt over 10 sts, sc in next 5 sc, 2 sc in next sc, sc in next 11 sc, 2 sc in next sc, sc in last 6 sc, join with sl st to beg sc, turn—2 sts inc'd.

Rnd 12: Ch 1, sc in each st around, join with sl st to beg sc, turn—49 sc.

Rnd 13 (Inc): Ch 1, sc in next 13 sc, work Row 15 of Right Hand Cable patt over 10 sts, sc in next 5 sc, 2 sc in next sc, sc in next 13 sc, 2 sc in next sc, sc in last 6 sc, join with sl st to beg sc, turn—2 sts inc'd.

Rnd 14: Ch 1, sc in each st around, join with sl st to beg sc, turn—51 sc.

Rnd 15: Ch 1, sc in next 13 sc, work Row 15 of Right Hand Cable patt (for a second time) over 10 sts, sc in last 28 sc, join with sl st to beg sc, turn.

Rnd 16: Ch 1, sc in each st around, join with sl st to beg sc, turn.

Rnd 17: Ch 1, sc in next 13 sc, work Row 15 of Right Hand Cable patt (for a third time) over 10 sts, sc in next 6 sc, sk next 14 sc, ch 1, sc in last 7 sc, join with sl st to beg sc, turn—37 sts.

Rnd 18: Ch 1, sc in each st around, join with sl st to beg sc, turn.

Upper Hand

Rnd 1: Ch 1, sc in each of next 9 (11, 13) sc, work Row 17 of Right Hand Cable patt over 10 sts, sc in last 10 (12, 14) sc, join with sl st to beg sc, turn.

Rnd 2: Ch 1, sc in each st around, join with sl st to beg sc, turn—29 (33, 37) sc.

Rnd 3: Ch 1, sc in next 9 (11, 13) sc, work Row 19 of Right Hand Cable patt over 10 sts, sc in last 10 (12, 14) sc, join with sl st to beg sc, turn—28 (32, 36) sts.

Rnd 4: Ch 1, sc in each st around, join with sl st to beg sc, turn.

Medium & Large Sizes Only

Rnds 5–6: Ch 1, sc in each st around, join with sl st to beg sc, turn.

All Sizes

Next rnd: Ch 1, work Crab Stitch patt around, join with sl st to beg sc. Fasten off.

Left Mitt

Ch 27 (31, 35). Join with sl st to bump of 1st ch to form ring, being careful not to twist chs.

Cuff

Rnd 1: Ch 1, working through bump of each ch, esc in same ch, esc in each ch around, join with sl st to form ring—27 (31, 35) esc.

Rnd 2: Ch 1, esc in same st, [fpdc in next st, esc in next st] 5 (6, 7) times, fpdc in each of next 6 sts, [esc in next st, fpdc in next st] 5 (6, 7) times, join with sl st to beg esc.

Rnds 3–6: Rep Rnd 2.

Hand

Begin working in joined rows.

Rnd 1: Ch 1, 2 sc in first sc, sc in next 8 (10, 12) sts, work Row 1 of Left Hand Cable patt over 10 sts, sc in each sc around, join with sl st to beg sc, turn—29 (33, 37) sc.

Rnd 2 (WS): Ch 1, sc in each st around, join with sl st to beg sc, turn.

Thumb Gusset

Rnd 1 (Inc): Ch 1, sc in next 4 (5, 6) sc, 2 sc in next sc, sc in next sc, 2 sc in next sc, sc in next 3 (4, 5) sc, work Row 3 of Left Hand Cable patt over 10 sts, sc in last 9 (11, 13) sc, join with sl st to beg sc, turn—2 sts inc'd.

Rnd 2 (WS): Ch 1, sc in each st around, join with sl st to beg sc, turn—31 (35, 39) sc.

Rnd 3 (Inc): Ch 1, sc in next 4 (5, 6) sc, 2 sc in next sc, sc in next 3 sc, 2 sc in next sc, sc in next 3 (4, 5) sc, work Row 5 of Left Hand Cable patt over 10 sts, sc in last 9 (11, 13) sc, join with sl st to beg sc, turn—2 sts inc'd.

Rnd 4: Ch 1, sc in each st around, join with sl st to beg sc, turn—33 (37, 41) sc.

Rnd 5 (Inc): Ch 1, sc in next 4 (5, 6) sc, 2 sc in next sc, sc in next 5 sc, 2 sc in next sc, sc in next 3 (4, 5) sc, work Row 7 of Left Hand Cable patt over 10 sts, sc in last 9 (11, 13) sc, join with sl st to beg sc, turn—2 sts inc'd.

Rnd 6: Ch 1, sc in each st around, join with sl st to beg sc, turn—35 (39, 43) sc.

Rnd 7 (Inc): Ch 1, sc in next 4 (5, 6) sc, 2 sc in next sc, sc in next 7 sc, 2 sc in next sc, sc in next 3 (4, 5) sc, work Row 9 of Left Hand Cable patt over 10 sts, sc in last 9 (11, 13) sc, join with sl st to beg sc, turn—2 sts inc'd.

Rnd 8: Ch 1, sc in each st around, join with sl st to beg sc, turn—37 (41, 45) sc.

Rnd 9 (Inc): Ch 1, sc in next 4 (5, 6) sc, 2 sc in next sc, sc in next 9 sc, 2 sc in next sc, sc in next 3 (4, 5) sc, work Row 11 of Left Hand Cable patt over 10 sts, sc in last 9 (11, 13) sc, join with sl st to beg sc, turn—2 sts inc'd.

Rnd 10: Ch 1, sc in st around, join with sl st to beg sc, turn—39 (43, 47) sc.

Small Size Only

Rnd 11: Ch 1, sc in next 20 sc, work Row 13 of Left Hand Cable patt over 10 sts, sc in last 9 sc, join with sl st to beg sc, turn.

Rnd 12: Ch 1, sc in each st around, join with sl st to beg sc, turn—39 sc.

Rnd 13: Ch 1, sc in next 5 sc, sk next 10 sc, ch 1, sc in next 4 sc, work Row 15 of Left Hand Cable patt over 10 sts, sc in last 9 sc, join with sl st to beg sc, turn—29 sts.

Rnd 14: Ch 1, sc in each st around, join with sl st to beg sc, turn.

Medium Size Only

Rnd 11 (Inc): Ch 1, sc in next 5 sc, 2 sc in next sc, sc in next 11 sc, 2 sc in next sc, sc in next 4 sc, work Row 13 of Left Hand Cable patt over 10 sts, sc in last 11 sc, join with sl st to beg sc, turn—2 sts inc'd.

Rnd 12: Ch 1, sc in each st around, join with sl st to beg sc, turn—45 sc.

Rnd 13: Ch 1, sc in next 24 sc, work Row 15 of Left Hand Cable patt over 10 sts, sc in last 11 sc, join with sl st to beg sc, turn.

Rnd 14: Ch 1, sc in each st around, join with sl st to beg sc, turn.

Rnd 15: Ch 1, sc in next 6 sc, sk next 12 sc, ch 1, sc in next 5 sc, ch 1, work Row 15 of Left Hand Cable patt (for a second time) over 10 sts, sc in last 11 sc, join with sl st to beg sc, turn—33 sts rem.

Rnd 16: Ch 1, sc in each st around, join with sl st to beg sc, turn.

Large Size Only

Rnd 11 (Inc): Ch 1, sc in next 6 sc, 2 sc in next sc, sc in each of next 11 sc, 2 sc in next sc, sc in next 5 sc, work Row 13 of Left Hand Cable patt over 10 sts, sc in each of last 13 sc, join with sl st to beg sc, turn—2 sts inc'd.

Rnd 12: Ch 1, sc in each st around, join with sl st to beg sc, turn—49 sc.

Rnd 13 (Inc): Ch 1, sc in next 6 sc, 2 sc in next sc, sc in next 13 sc, 2 sc in next sc, sc in next 5 sc, work Row 15 of Left Hand Cable patt over 10 sts, sc in last 13 sc, join with sl st to beg sc, turn—2 sts inc'd.

Rnd 14: Ch 1, sc in each st around, join with sl st to beg sc, turn—51 sc.

Rnd 15: Ch 1, sc in next 28 sc, work Row 15 of Left Hand Cable patt (for a second time) over 10 sts, sc in last 13 sc, join with sl st to beg sc, turn.

Rnd 16: Ch 1, sc in each st around, join with sl st to beg sc, turn.

Rnd 17: Ch 1, sc in next 7 sc, sk next 14 sc, ch 1, sc in next 6 sc, ch 1, work Row 15 of Left Hand Cable patt (for a third time) over 10 sts, sc in last 13 sc, join with sl st to beg sc, turn—37 sts.

Rnd 18: Ch 1, sc in each st around, join with sl st to beg sc, turn.

Upper Hand

Rnd 1: Ch 1, sc in next 10 (12, 14) sc, work Row 17 of Left Hand Cable patt over 10 sts, sc in last 9 (11, 13) sc, join with sl st to beg sc, turn.

Rnd 2: Ch 1, sc in each st around, join with sl st to beg sc, turn—29, (33, 37) sc.

Rnd 3: Ch 1, sc in next 10 (12, 14) sc, work Row 19 of Left Hand Cable patt over 10 sts, sc in last 9 (11, 13) sc, join with sl st to beg sc, turn—28 (32, 36) sts rem.

Rnd 4: Ch 1, sc in each st around, join with sl st to beg sc, turn.

Medium & Large Sizes Only

Rnds 5–6: Ch 1, sc in each st around, join with sl st to beg sc, turn.

All Sizes

Next rnd: Ch 1, work Crab Stitch patt around, join with sl st to beg sc. Fasten off.

Finishing

Join yarn to center of Thumb gap. Ch 1, work Crab Stitch patt around, join with sl st to beg sc. Fasten off. Weave in ends.

Little
Victory

Crocheted shells are not just for doilies! With a pretty yarn and bold black buttons, these long, lacy mitts take a traditional pattern and give it an updated look. Pull them to your elbows when things are chilly, or wear them slouchy for a casual look.

FINISHED MEASUREMENTS

Forearm: 7³/₄ (9, 10)"/19.5 (23, 25.5) cm
Hand circumference: 6¹/₄ (7¹/₄, 8¹/₄)"/16 (18.5, 21) cm
Length: 12¹/₂ (13, 13)"/32 (33, 33) cm
Note: This mitt is stretchy. Choose a size based on approximately 1"/2.5 cm less in circumference than your actual hand circumference.

SIZES

Women's Small (Medium, Large)
Shown in Small.

YARN

Fibra Natura Whisper Lace, super fine weight #1 yarn (70% wool, 30% silk; 440 yds/1.75 oz; 402 m/50 g)
• 1 skein #110 Lemongrass

HOOKS AND OTHER MATERIALS

• US B-1 (2.25 mm) crochet hook
• US steel 7 (1.65 mm) crochet hook
• Tapestry needle
• Fourteen ³/₈"/1 cm buttons

GAUGE

27 sts x 15 rows in Lacy Shells patt = 4"/10 cm square using larger hook
32 sts x 36 rows in sc = 4"/10 cm square using smaller hook
Be sure to check your gauge!

NOTES

• The arm is worked back and forth in rows, then joined in the round and worked in joined rows from the hand on.

STITCH GUIDE

Shell
Work 5 dcs into sp or st indicated.
Beg Shell
Work 3 dcs into sp or st indicated.

STITCH PATTERNS

Lacy Shells (worked in rows)
(multiple of 7 sts + 4)
Set-up row (WS): Ch 2, dc in 1st st, dc in next 2 sts, [sk next 2 sts, Shell in next st, sk next 2 sts, dc in next 2 sts] across, dc in last st, turn.
Row 1 (RS): Ch 2, dc in 1st dc, Beg Shell between next 2 dc, [dc between 2nd and 3rd dcs of next Shell, dc between 3rd and 4th dcs of same Shell, Shell between the pair of dcs] across, dc between 2nd and 3rd dcs of next Shell, dc bet 3rd and 4th dcs of same Shell, Shell between 2nd and 3rd dc from end, dc in last dc, turn.
Row 2 (WS): Ch 2, dc in 1st dc, dc between same dc and 1st dc of Beg Shell, dc between 1st and 2nd dc of Beg Shell, [Shell between the pair of dcs, dc between 2nd and 3rd dcs of next Shell, dc between 3rd and 4th dcs of same Shell] across, dc between 2nd and 3rd dc of Beg Shell, dc between 3rd dc of Beg Shell and last dc, dc in last dc, turn.
Rep Rows 1–2 for patt.

Lacy Shells (worked in joined rows)
(multiple of 7 sts)
Set-up row (WS): Ch 3 (counts as dc), [sk next 2 sts, Shell in next st, sk next 2 sts, dc in next 2 sts] across, sk next 2 sts, Shell in next st, sk next 2 sts, dc in last st, join with sl st to beg dc, turn.
Row 1 (RS): Sl st in sp between 1st and last dcs of previous row, ch 3 (counts as dc), Beg Shell in same sp, [dc between 2nd and 3rd dcs of next Shell, dc between 3rd and 4th dcs of same Shell, Shell between the pair of dcs] across, dc between 2nd and 3rd dcs of next Shell, dc in same sp as beg dc, join with sl st to beg dc, sl st in sp between same dc and next dc, turn.
Row 2 (WS): Ch 3 (counts as dc), [Shell between the pair of dcs, dc between 2nd and 3rd dcs of next Shell, dc between 3rd and 4th dcs of same Shell] across, end Shell between the pair of dcs, dc between 2nd and 3rd dcs of next Shell, join with sl st to beg dc, turn.
Rep Rows 1–2 for patt.

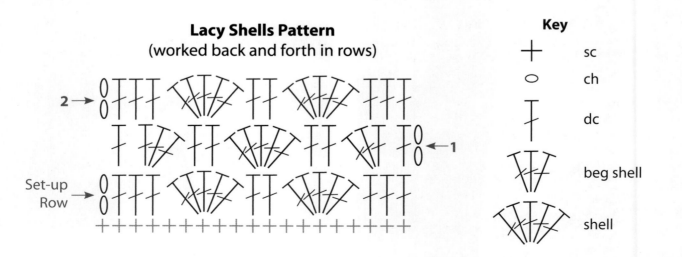

Lacy Shells Pattern
(worked back and forth in rows)

Key

+	sc
o	ch
⊤	dc
beg shell
shell

Right Mitt

Arm

With larger hook, ch 54 (61, 68).

Set-up row: Sc in 2nd ch from hook and each ch across, turn—53 (60, 67) sc.

Section 1

Work Set-up row of Lacy Shells patt worked in rows. Rep Rows 1–2 of Lacy Shells patt worked in rows 7 times, then rep Row 1.

Next row (WS): Ch 1, sc in 1st dc, fpdc in next dc and each dc to last dc, sc in last dc, turn.

Dec row 1 (RS): Ch 1, sc in 1st sc, bpsc in next 1 (2, 3) dc, [bpsc2tog, bpsc in next 6 (7, 8) dc] 6 times, bpsc2tog, sc in last sc, turn—7 sts dec'd, 46 (53, 60) sts.

Section 2

Work Set-up row of Lacy Shells patt worked in rows. Rep Rows 1–2 of Lacy Shells patt worked in rows 2 times, then rep Row 1.

Next row (WS): Ch 1, sc in 1st dc, fpdc in next dc and each dc to last dc, sc in last dc, turn.

Dec row 2 (RS): Ch 1, sc in 1st sc, bpsc in next dc, [bpsc2tog, bpsc in next 5 (6, 7) dc] 6 times, bpsc2tog, bpsc in next dc, sc in last sc, ch 3, join with sl st to beg sc—4 sts dec'd, 42 (49, 56) sts.

Fasten off.

Hand

With RS facing, count 16 (19, 22) sts to the left of 1st st of last row worked. Join yarn with sl st, turn.

Work Set-up row of Lacy Shells patt worked in joined rows. Work Rows 1–2 of Lacy Shells patt worked in joined rows, then rep Row 1.

Thumb Opening

Row 1 (WS): Ch 2, 3 dcs in same sp, [shell between the pair of dcs, dc between 2nd and 3rd dcs of next Shell, dc between 3rd and 4th dcs of same Shell] across, end shell between the pair of dcs, 3 dc between 3rd dc of Beg Shell and last dc, turn—2 sts inc'd, 44 (51, 58) sts.

Rep Rows 1–2 of Lacy Shells patt worked in rows 4 (5, 5) times, then rep Row 1.

Next row (WS): Sl st between next 2 dcs, ch 3 (counts as dc), [shell between the pair of dcs, dc between 2nd and 3rd dcs of next Shell, dc between 3rd and 4th dcs of same Shell], end Shell between the pair of dcs, dc between 3rd dc of next Shell and last dc, join with sl st to beg dc, sl st between dc just made and 1st dc, turn—42 (49, 56) sts.

Upper Hand

Work Rows 1–2 of Lacy Shells patt worked in joined rows 3 times.

Next row (RS): Work Row 1 of Lacy Shells patt to end, turn, sl st in next dc, turn.

Next rnd (RS): Ch 5, sk next 3 dc, sl st in next dc (last dc of shell), [sl st, hdc, dc, hdc, sl st] in sp between next 2 dc, {sl st in next dc (1st dc of shell), ch 5, sk next 3 dc, sl st in next dc (last dc of shell), [sl st, hdc, dc, hdc, sl st] in sp between next 2 dc} across. Fasten off.

Thumb

Attach yarn to upper edge of Thumb opening with larger hook.

Rnd 1: Ch 1, work 40 (48, 48) sc evenly around opening, about 2 sc for every row, join with sl st to beg sc.

Rnd 2: Ch 1, bpsc in same sc, bpsc in next 7 (9, 9) sc, bphdc in next 6 (7, 7) sc, bpdc in next 12 (14, 14) sc, bphdc in next 6 (7, 7) sc, bpsc in next 8 (10, 10) sc, join with sl st to beg sc.

Rnd 3: Ch 1, bpsc in same sc, bpsc in next 7 (9, 9) sc, bphdc in next 6 (7, 7) hdc, bpdc2tog, bpdc in next 2 (3, 3) dc, bptr in next 4 dc, bpdc in next 2 (3, 3) dc, bpdc2tog, bphdc in next 6 (7, 7) hdc, bpsc in next 8 (10, 10) sc, join with sl st to beg sc—2 sts dec'd.

Rnd 4: Loosely sl st in blo of each st around.

Fasten off.

Button Edging

With RS facing and smaller hook, attach yarn to lower LH side of opening at beg-ch edge.

Row 1 (RS): Ch 1, work 49 sc evenly along LH side of opening (about 2 sc for every dc row), 3 sc along upper edge of opening, and 49 sc evenly along RH side of opening, turn.

Row 2 (WS): Ch 1, sc in same sc, sc in next 47 sc, sc2tog, sc in next sc, sc2tog, sc in next 2 sc, [ch 7 (for button loop), sl st in last sc made, sc in next 7 sc] 6 times, ch 7, sl st in last sc made, sc in last 4 sc. Do not fasten off.

Upper Arm Edging

Row 1 (WS): Work 1 sc in same st as last sc of Row 2 of Button Edging, [dc, hdc] in bottom of 1st dc along Upper Arm, {[sl st, hdc, dc, hdc, sl st] in sp between next 2 dc, sl st between next dc and Shell, ch 5, sk next Shell, sl st between Shell and next dc} across, end [sl st, hdc, dc, hdc, sl st] in sp between next 2 dc, [hdc, dc] in last sc, sl st in same sc, turn.

Row 2 (RS): {Ch 7, [sl st, hdc, dc, hdc, sl st] in 3rd ch of next ch-5 sp} across, ch 7, sl st in last dc.

Fasten off.

Left Mitt

Arm

Work as for Right Mitt.

Hand

With RS facing, count 26 (30, 34) sts to the left of 1st st of last row worked. Join yarn with sl st, turn.

Complete Hand as for Right Mitt.

Thumb and Upper Hand

Complete as for Right Mitt.

Button Edging

With RS facing and smaller hook, attach yarn to lower LH side of opening at beg-ch edge.

Row 1 (RS): Ch 1, work 49 sc evenly along LH side of opening (about 2 sc for every dc row), 3 sc along upper edge of opening, and 49 sc evenly along RH side of opening, turn.

Row 2 (WS): Ch 1, sc in same sc, sc in next 3 sc, [ch 7 (for button loop), sl st in last sc made, sc in next 7 sc] 6 times, ch 7, sl st in last sc made, sc in next 2 sc, sc2tog, sc in next sc, sc2tog, sc in last 48 sc. Fasten off.

Upper Arm Edging

Work as for Right Mitt.

Finishing

Weave in ends. Wet block mitt to even out stitches and open up lace. Sew buttons to Button Edging opposite button loops.

Vegas, Baby!

Go big or go home. Girly lace meets a rough-and-tumble metal zipper in these bright lights, big city mitts. Faced with any challenge life might throw at you, these sparkly mitts are here to prove just one truth: attitude is everything.

FINISHED MEASUREMENTS
Palm circumference: $6^1/_4$ ($7^1/_2$)"/16 (19) cm
Note: These mitts are very stretchy. Choose a size up to 1"/2.5 cm smaller than your actual palm circumference.
Length: $5^1/_2$ (6)"/14 (15) cm

SIZES
Women's Small (Medium)
Shown in Small.

YARN
Premier Yarns Spangle, light weight #3 yarn (75% nylon, 25% metallic; 164 yds/1.75 oz; 150 m/50 g)
• 2 balls #11-208 Sparkling Water

HOOK AND OTHER MATERIALS
• US C-2 (2.75 mm) crochet hook
• Tapestry needle
• Two 7"/18 cm metal zippers (or longer; they will be trimmed)
• Sewing needle and thread
• Straight pins

GAUGE
26 sts x 16 rows in Shell Columns patt = 4"/10 cm square
Be sure to check your gauge!

STITCH GUIDE
Picot
[Sl st, ch 3, sl st] in st indicated.

STITCH PATTERN

Shell Columns (multiple of 4 sts + 3)

Row 1 (RS): Ch 1, dc in 1st dc, fptr around next tr from 2 rows below, sk dc behind fptr just made, [sk next dc, ch 1, dc in next dc, ch 1, sk next dc, fptr around next tr from 2 rows below, sk dc behind fptr just made] to last st, dc in last dc, turn.

Row 2 (WS): Ch 1, dc in 1st dc, [dc in next tr, 3 dc in next dc] to last 2 sts, dc in next tr, dc in last dc, turn.

Rep Rows 1–2 for patt.

Right Mitt

Ch 31 (37).

Cuff

Row 1 (RS): Sc in 2nd ch from hook and each ch across, turn—30 (36) sc.

Row 2 (WS): Ch 1, dc in each sc across, turn,

Row 3: Ch 1, dc in 1st dc, fptr around post of each dc across to last dc, dc in last dc, turn.

Row 4: Ch 1, dc in each st across, turn.

Row 5: Ch 1, dc in 1st dc, fptr around post of each tr from 2 rows below, dc in last dc, turn.

Row 6: Ch 1, dc in each st across, turn.

Rows 7–8: Rep Rows 5–6.

Small Size Only

Row 9 (Inc row): Ch 1, dc in 1st dc, [fptr around post of next tr from 2 rows below, sk dc behind fptr just made, ch 1, dc in next dc, ch 1, sk next dc, fptr around post of next tr from 2 rows below, sk dc behind fptr just made, sk next dc, ch 1, dc in next dc, ch 1] 3 times, [fptr around post of

next tr from 2 rows below, sk dc behind fptr just made, ch 1, dc in next dc, ch 1, sk next dc] 2 times, fptr around post of next tr from 2 rows below, sk dc behind fptr just made, dc in last dc, turn—5 sts inc'd, 35 sts; 9 fptr.

Medium Size Only

Row 9 (Inc row): Ch 1, dc in 1st dc, fptr around post of next tr from 2 rows below, sk dc behind fptr just made, ch 1, dc in next dc, ch 1, sk next dc, [fptr around post of next tr from 2 rows below, sk dc behind fptr just made, ch 1, dc in next dc, ch 1, sk next dc, fptr around post of next tr from 2 rows below, sk dc behind fptr just made, sk next dc, ch 1, dc in next dc, ch 1] 3 times, [fptr around post of next tr from 2 rows below, sk dc behind fptr just made, ch 1, dc in next dc, ch 1, sk next dc] 3 times, fptr around post of next tr from 2 rows below, sk dc behind fptr just made, dc in last dc, turn—7 sts inc'd, 43 sts; 11 fptr.

Hand

Set-up row (WS): Ch 1, dc in 1st dc, [dc in next tr, 3 dc in next dc] 8 (10) times, dc in next tr, dc in last dc, turn.

Work Rows 1–2 of Shell Columns patt 3 times.

Thumb Opening

Row 1 (RS): Ch 1, dc in 1st dc, fptr around next tr from 2 rows below, sk dc behind fptr just made [sk next dc, ch 1, dc in next dc, ch 1, sk next dc, fptr around next tr from 2 rows below, sk dc behind fptr just made] 2 (3) times, ch 11, sk next 11 dc, fptr around next tr from 2 rows below, sk dc behind fptr just made [sk next dc, ch 1, dc in next dc, ch 1, sk next dc, fptr around next tr from 2 rows below, sk dc behind fptr just made] 3 (4) times, dc in last dc, turn.

Shell Columns

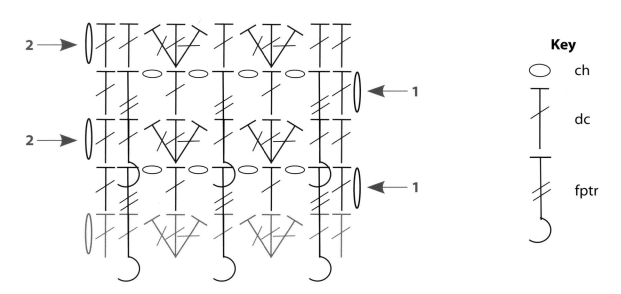

Key

○ ch

† dc

‡ fptr

Row 2: Ch 1, dc in 1st dc, [dc in next tr, 3 dc in next dc] 3 (4) times, dc in next tr, [sk next ch, 3 dc in next ch, sk next ch, dc in next ch] 2 times, sk next ch, 3 dc in next ch, sk last ch, [dc in next tr, 3 dc in next dc] 2 (3) times, dc in next tr, dc in last dc, turn.

Upper Hand

Row 1 (RS): Ch 1, dc in 1st dc, fptr around next tr from 2 rows below, sk dc behind fptr just made, [sk next dc, ch 1, dc in next dc, ch 1, sk next dc, fptr around next tr from 2 rows below, sk dc behind fptr just made] 2 (3) times, [sk next dc, ch 1, dc in next dc, ch 1, fptr around ch from 2 rows below, sk dc behind fptr just made] 2 times, [sk next dc, ch 1, dc in next dc, ch 1, sk next dc, fptr around next tr from 2 rows below, sk dc behind fptr just made] 4 (5) times, dc in last dc, turn.

Work Row 2 of Shell Columns patt, then rep Rows 1–2 of patt 2 (3) times.

Upper Edging

Note: Upper Edging is worked in joined rows.

Row 1 (RS): Work Row 1 of Shell Columns patt to end, ch 5, join to beg dc, turn—40 (48) sts.

Row 2 (WS): Ch 1, sk 1st dc, 3 dc in next ch, sk next ch, dc in next ch, sk next ch, 3 dc in next ch, sk next dc, [dc in next tr, 3 dc in next dc] across, end dc in last tr, join to beg dc, turn.

Row 3: Ch 1, [fptr around tr from 2 rows below, ch 1, sk next dc, dc in next dc, ch 1] 9 (10, 11) times, fptr around base of ch-1 below next dc, ch 1, sk next dc, dc in next dc, ch 1, join with sl st to beg tr, turn.

Row 4: Ch 1, dc in each st and sp across, join with sl st to beg dc, turn.

Row 5: Ch 1, [fptr in tr from 2 rows below, ch 1, sk dc behind tr just made, sk next dc, picot in next dc, ch 1, sk next dc] across, join with sl st to beg tr.

Fasten off.

Zipper Edging

With RS facing, attach yarn with sl st at lower edge of opening.

Row 1 (RS): Ch 1, work 24 (27) hdc evenly along left side of opening, 5 hdc along ch-5, 24 (27) hdc evenly along right side of opening, turn—53 (59) hdc.

Row 2 (WS): Working loosely, ch 1, sl st in next 23 (26) hdc, sl st next 2 hdc tog, sl st in next 3 hdc, sl st next 2 hdc tog, sl st in next 23 (26) hdc—51 (57) hdc.

Fasten off.

Thumb

With RS facing, attach yarn to right hand side of Thumb Opening.

Rnd 1 (RS): Ch 1, sc in same sp, working along lower edge of opening, sc in side of next tr, hdc in next 2 dc, dc in next 7 dc, hdc in next 2 dc, sc in side of next tr, sc in LH

side of Thumb Opening; working along upper edge of opening, sc in tr, sc in next 3 dc, sc in next tr, sc in next 3 dc, sc in next tr, sc in next 3 dc, sc in next tr, join with sl st to beg sc.

Rnd 2 (WS): Ch 1, sc loosely in each st around, join with sl st to beg sc.

Fasten off.

Left Mitt

Work as for Right Mitt to Thumb Opening.

Thumb Opening

Row 1 (RS): Ch 1, dc in 1st dc, fptr around next tr from 2 rows below, sk dc behind fptr just made, [sk next dc, ch 1, dc in next dc, ch 1, sk next dc, fptr around next tr from 2 rows below, sk dc behind fptr just made] 3 (4) times, ch 11, sk next 11 dc, fptr around next tr from 2 rows below, sk dc behind fptr just made, [sk next dc, ch 1, dc in next dc, ch 1, sk next dc, fptr around next tr from 2 rows below, sk dc behind fptr just made] 2 (3) times, dc in last dc, turn.

Row 2: Ch 1, dc in 1st dc, [dc in next tr, 3 dc in next dc] 2 (3) times, dc in next tr, [sk next ch, 3 dc in next ch, sk next ch, dc in next ch] 2 times, sk next ch, 3 dc in next ch, sk last ch, [dc in next tr, 3 dc in next dc] 3 (4) times, dc in next tr, dc in last dc, turn.

Upper Hand, Upper Edging, Zipper Edging, Thumb

Complete as for Right Mitt.

Finishing

Weave in ends. Lay zipper in opening so top stop is just visible underneath upper edge of opening. Leaving ³/₄"/2 cm at the end of zipper tape for folding under, trim zipper. Fold under ends of zipper and sew into place. Pin zipper into opening and sew onto Zipper Edging.

> **TIP:** **When sewing on a zipper, don't be shy with the pins! Straight pins will help hold your zipper while you sew it into place exactly where you want it. Take small, even stitches, and take your time.**

Adorn

Not quite mitts, these delicate hand adornments will complement a variety of outfits. They secure to your hand with just a middle finger loop and ball-and-loop-style wrist closure. Worked from the center out in a single piece, they're as fuss-free to crochet as they are to wear.

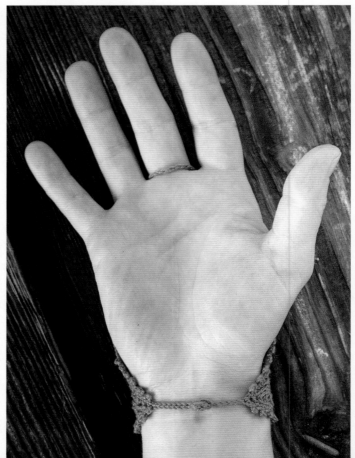

FINISHED MEASUREMENTS
Each edge of the triangular motif: $4^3/4$"/12 cm
Wrist: 7 ($7^3/4$, $8^1/4$)"/18 (20, 21) cm

SIZES
Women's Small (Medium, Large)
Shown in Small.

YARN
Nazli Gelin Garden 10, lace weight #0 yarn (100% mercerized Egyptian Giza cotton; 308 yds/1.75 oz; 282 m/50 g)
• 1 ball #700-17 (turquoise)

HOOK AND OTHER MATERIALS
• US steel 8 (1.5 mm) crochet hook
• Tapestry needle

GAUGE

Rnds 1–3 of motif = 1"/2.5 cm across

40 sts x 44 rows in sc = 4"/10 cm square

Be sure to check your gauge!

NOTES

- When working middle finger loop on Rnd 10 of motif, be sure to try on your finger before finishing the round. If the loop is too loose or too tight, remove or add chains as necessary to fit your finger.
- The motif is the same for each of the three sizes. The differences among the sizes are the circumferences of the middle finger loop and the lengths of the wrist closure.
- Rnd 10 of the motif chart refers to the smallest size for the middle finger loop, ball portion of closure, and loop portion of closure. For the two larger sizes, refer to the numbers in the written instructions.
- The only difference between Right and Left hands is Rnd 10 of the motif. The ball/loop closure on each hand is mirrored.

STITCH GUIDE

V-st

[Dc, ch 1, dc] in st indicated.

Picot

Ch 3, sl st in top of sc just made.

STITCH PATTERN

Motif

Ch 6, join with sl st to form ring.

Rnd 1: Ch 1, 12 sc in ring, join with sl st to beg sc.

Rnd 2: Ch 3 (counts as hdc + ch 1), {[hdc, ch 1] in next sc} around, join with sl st to 2nd ch of beg ch-3—12 hdc, 12 ch-1 sps.

Rnd 3: Ch 1, sc in same st, 2 sc in next ch-1 sp, sc in next hdc, sc in next ch-1 sp, [sc in next hdc, 2 sc in next ch-1 sp, sc in next hdc, sc in next ch-1 sp] around, join with sl st to beg sc—30 sc.

Rnd 4: Ch 5 (counts as tr + ch 1), sk 1st 2 sts, v-st in next st, ch 1, sk next st, dc in next st, ch 1, sk next st, v-st in next st, ch 1, sk next st, tr in next st, ch 5, sk next st, [tr in next st, ch 1, sk next st, v-st in next st, ch 1, sk next st, dc in next st, ch 1, sk next st, v st in next st, ch 1, sk next st, tr in next st, ch 5, sk next st] 2 times, join with sl st to 4th ch of beg ch-5.

Rnd 5: Ch 4 (counts as dc + ch 1), [dc in next dc, ch 1] 5 times, dc in next tr, ch 5, tr in ch-5 sp, ch 5, {dc in next tr, ch 1, [dc in next dc, ch 1] 5 times, dc in next tr, ch 5, tr in ch-5 sp, ch 5}} 2 times, join with sl st to 3rd ch of beg ch-4.

Rnd 6: Ch 4 (counts as dc + ch 1), [dc in next dc, ch 1] 5 times, dc in next dc, ch 5, dc in next ch-5 sp, ch 1, [tr, ch 1, tr] in next tr, ch 1, dc in next ch-5 sp, ch 5, {{dc in next dc, ch 1] 6 times, dc in next dc, ch 5, dc in next ch-5 sp, ch 1, [tr, ch 1, tr] in next tr, ch 1, dc in next ch-5 sp, ch 5}} 2 times, join with sl st to 3rd ch of beg ch-4.

Rnd 7: Ch 3 (counts as dc), dc in next 6 dc, ch 5, dc in next dc, ch 1, v-st in next ch-1 sp, ch 1, [tr, ch 1, tr] in next ch-1 sp, v-st in next ch-1 sp, ch 1, dc in next dc, ch 5, {dc in each of next 7 dc, ch 5, dc in next dc, ch 1, v-st in next ch-1 sp, ch 1, [tr, ch 1, tr] in next ch-1 sp, v-st in next ch-1 sp, ch 1, dc in next dc, ch 5} 2 times, join with sl st to top of beg ch-3.

Rnd 8: Ch 3 (counts as dc), [sk next dc, dc in next dc] 3 times, ch 7, dc in next dc, ch 1, v-st in next dc, ch 1, dc in next dc, ch 1, dc in next tr, ch 1, [tr, ch 1, tr] in next ch-1 sp, ch 1, dc in next tr, ch 1, dc in next dc, ch 1, v-st in next dc, ch 1, dc in next dc, ch 7, {dc in next dc, [sk next dc, dc in next dc] 3 times, ch 7, dc in next dc, ch 1, v-st in next dc, ch 1, dc in next dc, ch 1, dc in next tr, ch 1, [tr, ch 1, tr] in next ch-1 sp, ch 1, dc in next tr, ch 1, dc in next dc, ch 1, v-st in next dc, ch 1, dc in next dc, ch 7} 2 times, join with sl st to top of beg ch-3.

Rnd 9: {Sl st in sp bet next 2 dc, ch 3, dc2tog, ch 3, sl st in sp bet next 2 dc, 7 sc in ch-7 sp, [sc in next dc, sc in next ch-1 sp] 5 times, sc in next tr, [sc, ch 1, sc] in next ch-1 sp, sc in next tr, [sc in next ch-1 sp, sc in next dc] 5 times, 7 sc in ch-7 sp} 3 times, join with sl st to beg sl st.

Rnd 10: [Sc, hdc] in next ch-3 sp, v-st in top of dc2tog, [hdc, sc] in next ch-3 sp, sc in next 7 sc, [sc in next sc, picot, sc in next sc] 6 times, [sc, ch 25 (29, 33) for middle finger loop, sc] in ch-2 sp, [sc in each of next 2 sc, picot] 6 times, sc in next 7 sc, [sc, hdc] in next ch-3 sp, v-st in top of dc2tog, [hdc, sc] in next ch-3 sp, sc in next 7 sc, [sc in next sc, picot, sc in next sc] 6 times, [sc, ch 10 (12, 14), work 8 hdc into 2nd ch from hook, join with sl st to beg hdc (ball portion of closure made), sl st back down rem 8 chs from ch-10, sc] in ch-2 sp, [sc in next 2 sc, picot] 6 times, sc in next 7 sc, [sc, hdc] in next ch-3 sp, v-st in top of dc2tog, [hdc, sc] in next ch-3 sp, sc in next 7 sc, [sc in next sc, picot, sc in next sc] 6 times, [sc, ch 15 (17, 19), sl st in 6th ch from hook (loop portion of closure made) and each ch to base of ch-14, sc] in ch-2 sp, [sc in next 2 sc, picot] 6 times, sc in next 7 sc, join with sl st to beg sc.

Fasten off.

Right Hand

Work Rnds 1–10 of Motif patt.

Left Hand

Work Rnds 1–9 of Motif patt.

Rnd 10: [Sc, hdc] in next ch-3 sp, v-st in top of dc2tog, [hdc, sc] in next ch-3 sp, sc in next 7 sc, [sc in next sc, picot, sc in next sc] 6 times, [sc, ch 25 (29, 33) for middle finger loop, sc] in ch-2 sp, [sc in next 2 sc, picot] 6 times, sc in next 7 sc, [sc, hdc] in next ch-3 sp, v-st in top of dc2tog, [hdc, sc] in next ch-3 sp, sc in next 7 sc, [sc in next sc, picot, sc in next sc] 6 times, [sc, ch 15 (17, 19), sl st in 6th ch from hook (loop portion of closure made) and each ch to base of ch-14, sc] in ch-2 sp, [sc in next 2 sc, picot] 6 times, sc in next 7 sc, [sc, hdc] in next ch-3 sp, v-st in top of dc2tog, [hdc, sc] in next ch-3 sp, sc in next 7 sc, [sc in next sc, picot, sc in next sc] 6 times, [sc, ch 10 (12, 14), work 8 hdc into 2nd ch from hook, join with sl st to beg hdc (ball portion of closure made), sl st back down rem 8 chs from ch-10, sc] in ch-2 sp, [sc in next 2 sc, picot] 6 times, sc in next 7 sc, join with sl st to beg sc.

Finishing

Weave in ends. Steam or wet block, pinning out picots from final round. To wear, slide middle finger loop around middle finger, then push ball closure through loop.

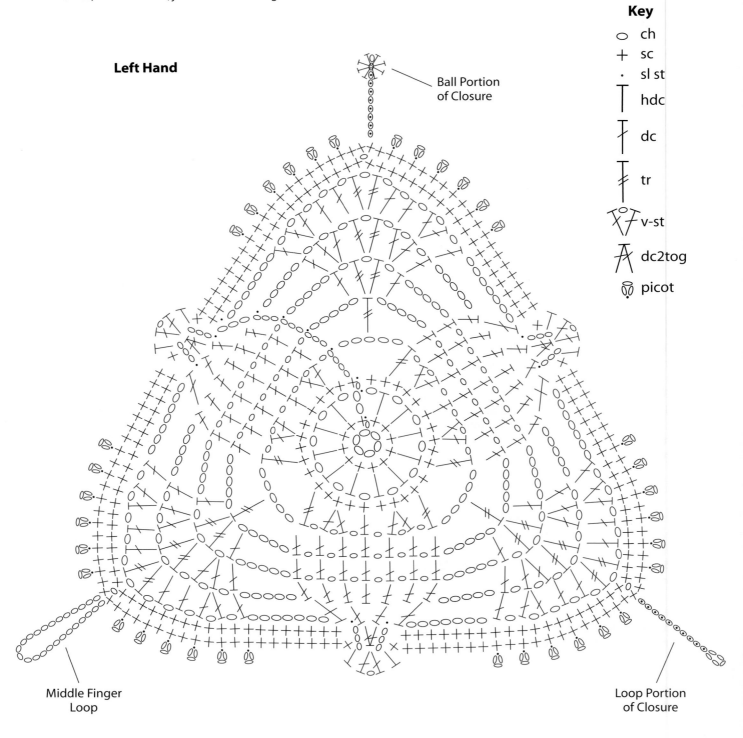

Left Hand

Ball Portion of Closure

Middle Finger Loop

Loop Portion of Closure

Key

○ ch
+ sc
· sl st
T hdc
dc
tr
v-st
dc2tog
picot

Right Hand

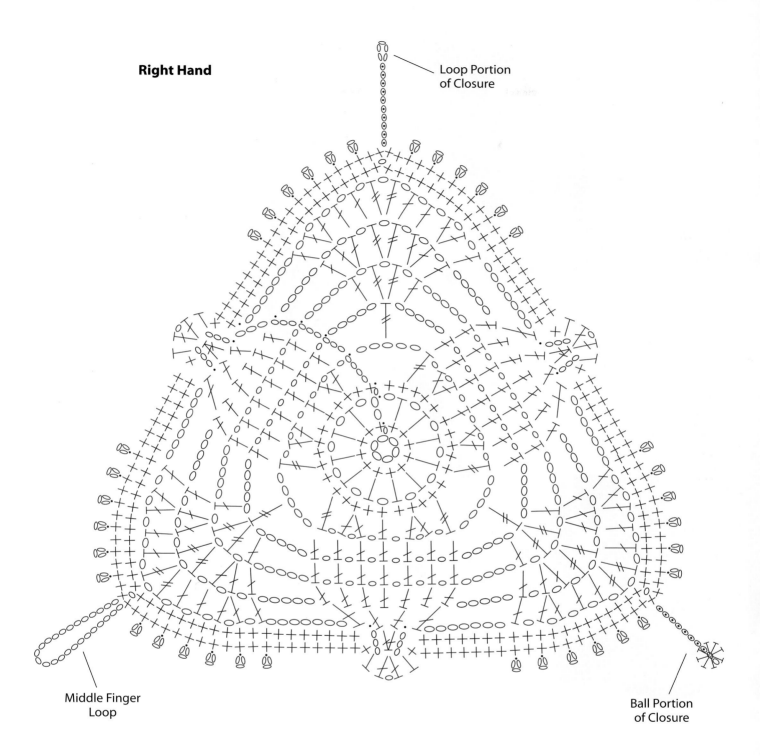

Loop Portion
of Closure

Middle Finger
Loop

Ball Portion
of Closure

Raindrops

These mitts present the perfect opportunity for you to unleash your creativity. Raindrops would look awesome with a striping yarn used for the main color and brightly contrasting colors for the applied lines and circles. For a very subtle textured effect, try using just a single color for all elements. Play around with the lengths of the applied crochet lines, or come up with a completely different design!

FINISHED MEASUREMENTS
Palm circumference: 7^1/$_2$"/19 cm (stretches to 12"/30.5 cm)
Length: 7^3/$_4$"/19.5 cm

SIZE
One size
Note: This mitt is very stretchy and is designed to fit a wide range of hand sizes.

YARN
Deborah Norville Collection Everyday Soft Worsted by Premier Yarns, medium weight #4 yarn (100% anti-pilling acrylic; 203 yds/4 oz; 186 m/113 g)
• 1 ball #ED100-40 Hot Fuchsia (MC)
• 1 ball #ED100-21 Magenta (CC1)
• 1 ball #ED100-32 Peony (CC2)

HOOKS AND OTHER MATERIALS

- US I-9 (5.5 mm) crochet hook
- US 7 (4.5 mm) crochet hook
- 8 removable stitch markers
- Tapestry needle

GAUGE

17 sts x 26 rows in slip stitch crochet = 4"/10 cm square
Be sure to check your gauge!

NOTES

- This mitt is worked entirely in slip stitch, through the back loop. Be sure to keep your tension loose and even, otherwise the stitches will be tight and difficult to work through. If you normally tension yarn by wrapping the yarn a couple of times around your finger, try wrapping only once, or not at all.
- See page 138 for a photo tutorial on applied crochet lines and circles.

Right Mitt

With MC and larger hook, ch 39.
Row 1 (RS): Sl st in blo of 2nd ch from hook and in blo of each ch across, turn—38 sl sts.
Row 2 (WS): Ch 1, sl st in blo of each sl st across, turn.
Rows 3–4: Rep Row 2. Place removable marker (marker 1) on RS of work between Rows 3 and 4.
Rows 5–10: Rep Row 2. Place removable marker (marker 2) on RS of work between Rows 9 and 10.
Rows 11–16: Rep Row 2. Place removable marker (marker 3) on RS of work between Rows 15 and 16.
Rows 17–22: Rep Row 2. Place removable marker (marker 4) on RS of work between Rows 21 and 22.
Rows 23–24: Rep Row 2.
Row 25: Ch 1, sl st in next 8 sl sts, ch 10 (for thumb opening), sk next 10 sl sts, sl st in last 20 sl sts, turn.
Row 26: Ch 1, sl st in next 20 sl sts, sl st through back lp and bottom bump of next 10 chs, sl st in last 8 sl sts, turn.
Rows 27–28: Rep Row 2. Place removable marker (marker 5) on RS of work between Rows 27 and 28.
Rows 29–34: Rep Row 2. Place removable marker (marker 6) on RS of work between Rows 33 and 34.
Rows 35–40: Rep Row 2. Place removable marker (marker 7) on RS of work between Rows 39 and 40.
Rows 41–46: Rep Row 2. Place removable marker (marker 8) on RS of work between Rows 45 and 46.
Rows 47–48: Rep Row 2.
Fasten off, leaving 24"/61 cm tail.

Applied Crochet Lines

Marker 1: With CC1 and smaller hook, work an applied crochet line over the first 22 sts between Rows 3 and 4, then work an applied crochet circle. Fasten off.

Markers 3, 5, 7: With CC1 and smaller hook, work applied crochet lines over the first 25 (31, 24) sts between rows indicated, then work an applied crochet circle. Fasten off.
Markers 2, 4, 6, 8: With CC2 and smaller hook, work applied crochet lines over the first 30 (20, 27, 32) sts between rows indicated, then work an applied crochet circle. Fasten off.

Thumb

Join MC to lower edge of thumb opening. With larger hook, working through blo of each sl st, sl st evenly around opening. Fasten off.

Left Mitt

Work as for Right Mitt.

Applied Crochet Lines

Note: Applied Crochet Lines for Left Mitt are worked as a mirror image to Right Mitt (see diagrams).
Marker 1: With CC2 and smaller hook, work an applied crochet line over the first 32 sts between Rows 3 and 4, then work an applied crochet circle. Fasten off.
Markers 3, 5, 7: With CC2 and smaller hook, work applied crochet lines over the first 27 (20, 30) sts between rows indicated, then work an applied crochet circle. Fasten off.

Diagram for Applied Crochet Lines

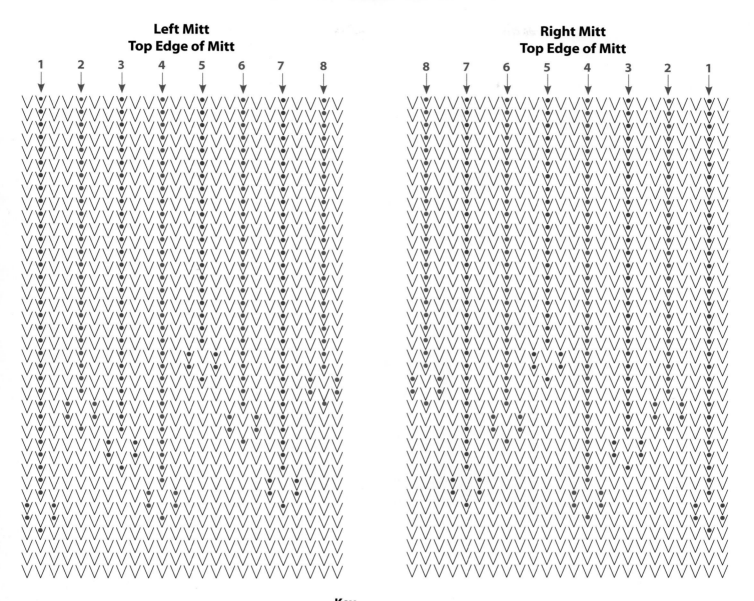

**Left Mitt
Top Edge of Mitt**

1 2 3 4 5 6 7 8

**Right Mitt
Top Edge of Mitt**

8 7 6 5 4 3 2 1

Key

- • sl st with CC1
- • sl st with CC2

Markers 2, 4, 6, 8: With CC1 and smaller hook, work applied crochet lines over the first 24 (31, 25, 22) sts between rows indicated, then work an applied crochet circle. Fasten off.

Thumb

Work as for Right Mitt.

Finishing

Join Row 48 to beg-ch side of Mitt using mattress stitch.

Upper Edging

With smaller hook, join CC1 to upper edge with sl st.
Rnd 1: Work 1 sl st in the side of each row around. Weave in all ends.

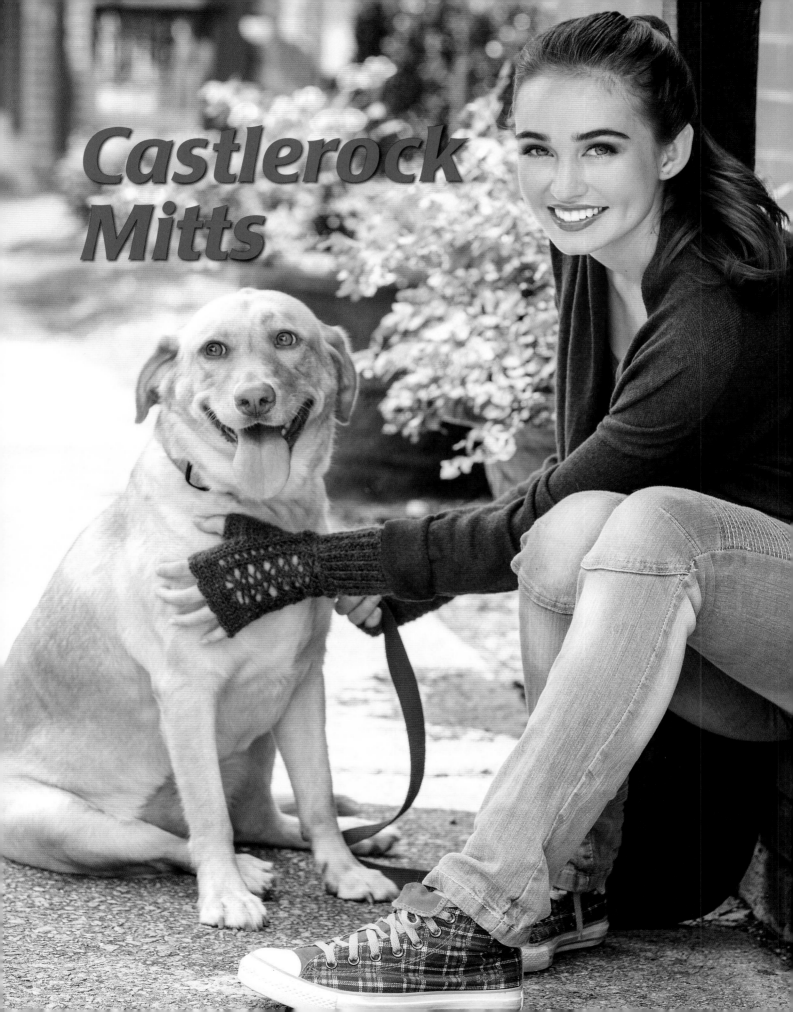

Castlerock Mitts

These mitts are a great way to try out a traditional technique—hairpin lace—for a modern look. For this method, loops are made on a narrow metal loom—the hairpin—and then are joined in the center using a crochet hook. You can find hairpin lace looms at your local craft store and online.

FINISHED MEASUREMENTS
Hand circumference: $7^{1}/_{4}$ (8, $8^{3}/_{4}$)"/18.5 (20.5, 22) cm
Length: $8^{3}/_{4}$ ($9^{1}/_{2}$, $10^{1}/_{4}$)"/22 (24, 26) cm

SIZES
Women's Small (Medium, Large)
Shown in Small.

YARN
Deborah Norville Collection Alpaca Dance by Premier Yarns, light weight #3 yarn (75% acrylic, 25% alpaca; 371 yds/3.5 oz; 340 m/100 g)
• 1 skein #25-11 Cinder

HOOK AND OTHER MATERIALS

- US D-3 (3.25 mm) crochet hook
- Adjustable hairpin lace loom with a width of 1¹/₂"/3.75 cm
- Smooth waste yarn in a contrasting color
- Tapestry needle

GAUGE

20 sts x 24 rows in sc = 4"/10 cm square
20 sts x 16 rows in sc = 4"/10 cm square
Be sure to check your gauge!

NOTES

- To construct these mitts, first a single strip of hairpin lace is made. Edging is worked on each side of the strip and the piece is set aside. The cuff is worked separately in the round. The hand is worked back and forth in rows, joining to the hairpin lace strip as you go. The strip is joined to the hand with a sl st at the beginning and end of each right side row.
- For a photo tutorial on hairpin lace, see page 144.

STITCH GUIDE

Extended Single Crochet (esc)
Insert hook into st indicated and pull up a lp (2 lps on hook), ch 1, yo, and pull through both lps on hook.

Right Mitt

Set hairpin lace loom to 1¹/₂"/3.75 cm width. (On a Susan Bates loom, this will be the center 2 positions for the aluminum bars). Make a hairpin lace strip that has 13 (15, 17) loops on each side. Fasten off. Slide a piece of waste yarn through each side of loops.

Strip Edging, Left Edge

Join yarn with sl st to first loop on the RH side of one long edge of strip.

Row 1 (RS): Ch 1, sc in same lp, [ch 1, sk next lp, sc in next lp, ch 1, sc in skipped lp] 6 (7, 8) times, turn—13 (15, 17) sc, 12 (14, 16) ch-1 sps. Remove waste yarn.

Row 2 (WS): Ch 1, sc in same sc, sc in each ch-1 sp and sc across, turn—25 (29, 33) sc.

Row 3: Ch 4 (counts as dc + ch 1), sk next sc, dc in next sc, [ch 1, sk next sc, dc in next dc] across, ending dc in last sc, turn—13 (15, 17) dc, 12 (14, 16) ch-1 sps.

Row 4: Ch 1, sc in same dc, sc in each ch-1sp and dc across, ending sc in 3rd ch of ch-4. Fasten off.

Strip Edging, Right Edge

With RS facing, join yarn with sl st to 2nd lp from RH side on opposite long edge of strip.

Row 1 (RS): Ch 1, sc in same loop, ch 1, sc in first (skipped) loop, [ch 1, sk next loop, sc in next loop, ch 1, sc in skipped loop] 5 (6, 7) times, ch 1, sc in last loop, turn—13 (15, 17) sc, 12 (14, 16) ch-1 sps.

Rows 2–3: Work as for Right Edging.

Row 4: Ch 1, sc in same dc, sc in each ch-1sp and dc across, ending sc in 3rd ch of ch-4, ch 1, sc in same st as last sc, turning 90 degrees and working along end of strip, work 2 sc into side of dc, sc in sides of each of next 2 rows, ch 3, hdc into center of strip, ch 3, sc in sides of each of next 2 rows from Left Edging, work 2 sc into side of dc, sc in same st as next sc, ch 1, join with sl st to next sc. Fasten off.

The strip now has edging on the left side, right side, and bottom. The bottom edging consists of 17 sts. Each side edging consists of 25 (29, 33) sts.

Cuff

Ch 32 (36, 40). Join with sl st to bump of 1st ch to form ring, being careful not to twist chs.

Rnd 1: Ch 1, working through bump of each ch, esc in same ch, esc in each ch around, join with sl st to form ring—32 (36, 40) esc.

Rnd 2: Ch 1, esc in same st, fpdc in next st, [esc in next st, fpdc in next st] around, join with sl st to beg esc.

Rnds 3–12: Rep Rnd 2.

Hand

Begin working back and forth in joined rows.
Hold strip with RS facing.

Row 1 (RS): Ch 1, sl st same st tog with first st from bottom edging of strip (working through flo of strip st), [sl st next cuff st tog with next st from bottom edging] 16 times, sl st in flo of first st from left side of strip edging, esc in next cuff st, 2 esc in next st, esc in each of next 3 (4, 5) sts, 2 esc in next st, esc in each of next 3 (5, 7) sts, 2 esc in next st, esc in each of next 3 (4, 5) sts, 2 esc in next st, esc in last st, join with sl st in flo of first st from right side of strip edging, turn—19 (23, 27) sts.

Row 2 (WS): Do not ch 1, sc in each st across, turn.

Row 3: Sk next st from left side of strip edging, sl st in flo of next st, esc in each st across, sk next st from right side of strip edging, sl st in flo of next st, turn.

Row 4: Sc in each st across, turn.

Rows 5–8: [Rep Rows 3–4] 2 times.

Thumb Gusset

Row 1 (RS): Sk next st from left side of strip edging, sl st in flo of next st, esc in next 3 (4, 5) sts, [2 esc in next sc] 2 times, esc in rem 14 (17, 20) sts, sk next st from right side of strip edging, sl st in flo of next st, turn—2 sts inc'd.

Row 2 (WS): Sc in next 14 (17, 20) sts, 2 sc in next st, sc in next 2 sts, 2 sc in next st, sc in last 3 (4, 5) sts, turn—2 sts inc'd, 23 (27, 31) sc.

Row 3: Sk next st from left side of strip edging, sl st in flo of next st, esc in next 3 (4, 5) sts, 2 esc in next sc, esc in next 4 sts, 2 esc in next sc, esc in rem 14 (17, 20) sts, sk next st from right side of strip edging, sl st in flo of next st, turn—2 sts inc'd.

Row 4: Sc in each st across, turn—25 (29, 33) sc.

Medium & Large Sizes Only

Row 13: Sk next st from left side of strip edging, sl st in flo of next st, esc in next 4 (5) sts, 2 esc in next sc, esc in next 14 sts, 2 esc in next sc, esc in rem 17 (20) sts, sk next st from right side of strip edging, sl st in flo of next st, turn—2 sts inc'd.

Row 14: Sc in each st across, turn—39 (43) sc.

Large Size Only

Row 15: Sk next st from left side of strip edging, sl st in flo of next st, esc in next 5 sts, 2 esc in next sc, esc in next 16 sts, 2 esc in next sc, esc in rem 20 sts, sk next st from right side of strip edging, sl st in flo of next st, turn—2 sts inc'd.

Row 16: Sc in each st across, turn—45 sc.

All Sizes

Next row (RS): Sk next st from left side of strip edging, sl st in flo of next st, esc in next 4 (5, 6) sts, sk next 14 (16, 18) sts, esc in last 15 (18, 21) sts, sk next st from right side of strip edging, sl st in flo of next st, turn—19 (23, 27) sts.

Next row (WS): Sc in each st across, turn.

Upper Hand

Row 1 (RS): Sk next st from left side of strip edging, sl st in flo of next st, esc in each st across, sk next st from right side of strip edging, sl st in flo of next st, turn.

Row 2 (WS): Sc in each st across, turn.

[Rep Rows 1–2] 0 (1, 2) more time(s), then rep Row 1. Strip edging is now entirely joined to the Hand.

Next row (WS): Sc in next 19 (23, 27) sts, sc in next sc from top of strip, work 2 sc into side of dc, sc in sides of each of next 2 rows, ch 3, hdc into center of strip, ch 3, sc in sides of each of next 2 rows from strip edging, work 2 sc into side of dc, sc in next sc, join with sl st to first sc of row, turn—36 (40, 44) sc.

Next row: Ch 1, esc in each st around, join with sl st to beg esc, turn—36 (40, 44) esc.

Next row: Ch 1, sc in each st around, join with sl st to beg sc, turn.

Next row: Ch 1, esc in each st around, join with sl st to beg esc, turn.

Top Edging

Row 1 (WS): Ch 1, sc in next st, [ch 2, sk next 2 sts, sc in next 2 sts] 8 (9, 10) times, ch 2, sk next 2 sts, sc in last st, join with sl st to beg sc, turn.

Row 2 (RS): Ch 1, sl st in next sc, [4 sc in ch-2 sp, sl st in next 2 sc] 8 (9, 10) times, 4 sc in next ch-2 sp, sl st in last sc, join with sl st to beg sl st. Fasten off.

Thumb

Note: Thumb is worked in joined rows.
Attach yarn to center of Thumb gap.

Row 5: Sk next st from left side of strip edging, sl st in flo of next st, esc in next 3 (4, 5) sts, 2 esc in next sc, esc in next 6 sts, 2 esc in next sc, esc in rem 14 (17, 20) sts, sk next st from right side of strip edging, sl st in flo of next st, turn—2 sts inc'd.

Row 6: Sc in each st across, turn—27 (31, 35) sc.

Row 7: Sk next st from left side of strip edging, sl st in flo of next st, esc in next 3 (4, 5) sts, 2 esc in next sc, esc in next 8 sts, 2 esc in next sc, esc in rem 14 (17, 20) sts, sk next st from right side of strip edging, sl st in flo of next st, turn—2 sts inc'd.

Row 8: Sc in each st across, turn—29 (33, 37) sc.

Row 9: Sk next st from left side of strip edging, sl st in flo of next st, esc in next 3 (4, 5) sts, 2 esc in next sc, esc in next 10 sts, 2 esc in next sc, esc in rem 14 (17, 20) sts, sk next st from right side of strip edging, sl st in flo of next st, turn—2 sts inc'd.

Row 10: Sc in each st across, turn—31 (35, 39) sc.

Row 11: Sk next st from left side of strip edging, sl st in flo of next st, esc in next 3 (4, 5) sts, 2 esc in next sc, esc in next 12 sts, 2 esc in next sc, esc in rem 14 (17, 20) sts, sk next st from right side of strip edging, sl st in flo of next st, turn—2 sts inc'd.

Row 12: Sc in each st across, turn—33 (37, 41) sc.

Row 1 (RS): Ch 1, esc in same sp, esc in next 14 (16, 18) Thumb sts, esc in sp in Thumb gap, join with sl st to beg esc, turn—16 (18, 20) esc.

Row 2 (WS): Ch 1, sc2tog, sc in next 12 (14, 16) sts, sc2tog, join with sl st to beg sc2tog, turn—14 (16, 18) sts.

Row 3: Ch 1, loosely sl st in each st around, join with sl st to beg sl st.

Left Mitt

Work as for Right Mitt to Thumb Gusset.

Thumb Gusset

Row 1 (RS): Sk next st from left side of strip edging, sl st in flo of next st, esc in next 14 (17, 20) sts, [2 esc in next sc] 2 times, esc in rem 3 (4, 5) sts, sk next st from right side of strip edging, sl st in flo of next st, turn—2 sts inc'd.

Row 2 (WS): Sc in next 3 (4, 5) sts, 2 sc in next st, sc in next 2 sts, 2 sc in next st, sc in last 14 (17, 20) sts, turn—2 sts inc'd, 23 (27, 31) sc.

Row 3: Sk next st from left side of strip edging, sl st in flo of next st, esc in next 14 (17, 20) sts, 2 esc in next sc, esc in next 4 sts, 2 esc in next sc, esc in rem 3 (4, 5) sts, sk next st from right side of strip edging, sl st in flo of next st, turn—2 sts inc'd.

Row 4: Sc in each st across, turn—25 (29, 33) sc.

Row 5: Sk next st from left side of strip edging, sl st in flo of next st, esc in next 14 (17, 20) sts, 2 esc in next sc, esc in next 6 sts, 2 esc in next sc, esc in rem 3 (4, 5) sts, sk next st from right side of strip edging, sl st in flo of next st, turn—2 sts inc'd.

Row 6: Sc in each st across, turn—27 (31, 35) sc.

Row 7: Sk next st from left side of strip edging, sl st in flo of next st, esc in next 14 (17, 20) sts, 2 esc in next sc, esc in next 8 sts, 2 esc in next sc, esc in rem 3 (4, 5) sts, sk next st from right side of strip edging, sl st in flo of next st, turn—2 sts inc'd.

Row 8: Sc in each st across, turn—29 (33, 37) sc.

Row 9: Sk next st from left side of strip edging, sl st in flo of next st, esc in next 14 (17, 20) sts, 2 esc in next sc, esc in next 10 sts, 2 esc in next sc, esc in rem 3 (4, 5) sts, sk next st from right side of strip edging, sl st in flo of next st, turn—2 sts inc'd.

Row 10: Sc in each st across, turn—31 (35, 39) sc.

Row 11: Sk next st from left side of strip edging, sl st in flo of next st, esc in next 14 (17, 20) sts, 2 esc in next sc, esc in next 12 sts, 2 esc in next sc, esc in rem 3 (4, 5) sts, sk next st from right side of strip edging, sl st in flo of next st, turn—2 sts inc'd.

Row 12: Sc in each st across, turn—33 (37, 41) sc.

Medium & Large Sizes Only

Row 13: Sk next st from left side of strip edging, sl st in flo of next st, esc in next 17 (20) sts, 2 esc in next sc, esc in next 14 sts, 2 esc in next sc, esc in rem 4 (5) sts, sk next st from right side of strip edging, sl st in flo of next st, turn—2 sts inc'd.

Row 14: Sc in each st across, turn—39 (43) sc.

Large Size Only

Row 15: Sk next st from left side of strip edging, sl st in flo of next st, esc in next 20 sts, 2 esc in next sc, esc in next 16 sts, 2 esc in next sc, esc in rem 5 sts, sk next st from right side of strip edging, sl st in flo of next st, turn—2 sts inc'd.

Row 16: Sc in each st across, turn—45 sc.

All Sizes

Next row (RS): Sk next st from left side of strip edging, sl st in flo of next st, esc in next 15 (18, 21) sts, sk next 14 (16, 18) sts, esc in last 4 (5, 6) sts, sk next st from right side of strip edging, sl st in flo of next st, turn—19 (23, 27) sts rem.

Next row (WS): Sc in each st across, turn.

Upper Hand, Top Edging, Thumb

Work as for Right Mitt.

Finishing

Weave in ends.

Houndstooth
Hands

Tapestry crochet never looked so stylish as in these houndstooth-patterned mittens. Crocheted in a worsted weight yarn, this is a great first tapestry crochet project; the yarn is heavy enough that it isn't fiddly. When choosing colors, try a main color that matches your favorite winter coat and a fun contrasting color for pop!

FINISHED MEASUREMENTS
Cuff circumference: $6^1/_4$ ($7^1/_2$, $8^3/_4$)"/16 (19, 22) cm
Hand circumference: 8 (9, 10)"/20.5 (23, 25.5) cm
Length: 10"/25.5 cm

YARN
Universal Yarn Deluxe Worsted, medium weight #4 yarn (100% wool; 220 yds/3.5 oz; 201 m/100 g)
• 1 skein #40004 Pewter (MC)
• 1 skein #12284 Strip Light Yellow (CC)

HOOKS AND OTHER MATERIALS
• US F-5 (3.75 mm) crochet hook
• US 7 (4.5 mm) crochet hook
• Tapestry needle

GAUGE
16 sts x 18 rows in Houndstooth patt = 4"/10 cm square using larger hook
Be sure to check your gauge!

NOTES

- The Houndstooth pattern is worked using the tapestry crochet method; see page 134 for a photo tutorial.
- When working the last stitch of the round in the Houndstooth pattern, end the stitch as follows: if the first stitch of the next row is the same color as the stitch just worked, end the stitch with the same color; if the color of the first stitch of the next row is not the same as the stitch just worked, end the stitch with the other color.

Right Mitten

Cuff

With MC and smaller hook, ch 12.

Set-up row (RS): Hdc in 2nd ch from hook and each ch across, turn—11 hdc.

Row 1 (WS): Ch 1, hdc in back bar of 1st hdc, ch 1, sk next hdc, hdc in back bar of next 9 hdc, turn.

Row 2 (RS): Ch 1, hdc in blo of 1st hdc, hdc in blo of next 8 hdc, hdc in blo of ch-1, hdc in blo of last hdc, turn.

[Rep Rows 1–2] 8 (9, 10) times, then rep Row 1—10 (11, 12) ch-1 sps.

Fasten off, leaving 8"/20 cm tail. Sew beg-ch edge to final row using mattress stitch.

Hand

Join MC to seam using larger hook.

Rnd 1: With MC, work 32 (36, 40) sc evenly along edge of Cuff.

Work Rows 1–4 of Houndstooth patt 2 times.

Thumb Opening

Rnd 1: Work Row 1 of Houndstooth patt over 1st 24 (26, 29) sts; ch 8 (9, 9), changing colors in patt as established, sk next 8 (9, 9) sts, work in patt over last 0 (0, 1) st, join with sl st to beg sc.

Rnd 2: Work Row 2 of Houndstooth patt over 1st 24 (26, 29) sc; working around yarn floats, work in patt over next 8 (9, 9) chs, work in patt to end.

Upper Hand

Work Rows 3–4 of Houndstooth patt.

[Work Rows 1–4 of Houndstooth patt] 3 (3, 4) times. Break CC.

Note: Remainder of Mitten is worked in a spiral. Do not join rnds.

Next rnd: With MC, ch 1, sc in blo of same st and each sc around, do not join. Rep this rnd 3 (5, 3) more times.

**Houndstooth
Pattern**

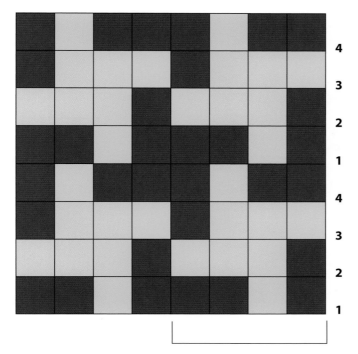

4
3
2
1
4
3
2
1

4 st rep

Key

 sc in blo with MC

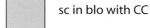 sc in blo with CC

Shape Top

Note: Work through blo of each sc.

Rnd 1: [Sc in next 6 (7, 8) sc, sc2tog] 4 times—4 sc dec'd, 28 (32, 36) sc.

Rnd 2: Sc in each sc around.

Rnd 3: Sc in next 2 (3, 3) sc, [sc2tog, sc in next 5 (6, 7) sc] 3 times, sc2tog, sc in last 3 (3, 4) sc—4 sc dec'd, 24 (28, 32) sc.

Rnd 4: [Sc in next 4 (5, 6) sc, sc2tog] 4 times—4 sc dec'd, 20 (24, 28) sc.

Rnd 5: Sc in next 1 (2, 2) sc, [sc2tog, sc in next 3 (4, 5) sc] 3 times, sc2tog, sc in last 2 (2, 3) sc—4 sc dec'd, 16 (20, 24) sc.

Rnd 6: [Sc in next 2 (3, 4) sc, sc2tog] 4 times—4 sc dec'd, 12 (16, 20) sc.

Rnd 7: [Sc2tog] around. Fasten off, leaving 8"/20 cm tail. Weave tail in and out of rem sts, pull taut.

Thumb

With larger hook and RS facing, attach MC to right side of Thumb Opening.

Rnd 1: Working along lower edge of opening, sc in blo of 1st 7 (8, 8) sc, sc2tog (next sc with thumb gap sp), sc in next 7 (8, 8) chs, sc2tog (last ch with thumb gap sp), do not join—16 (18, 18) sc.

Rnds 2–14: Sc in blo of each sc around.

Rnd 15: [Sc2tog] around. Fasten off, leaving 6"/15 cm tail. Weave tail in and out of rem sts, pull taut.

Left Mitten

Work as for Right Mitten to Thumb opening.

Thumb Opening

Rnd 1: Ch 1, work in patt over 0 (0, 1) sc, ch 8 (9, 9), changing colors as though in patt, sk next 8 (9, 9) sc, work in patt over rem 24 (26, 29) sc, join with sl st to beg ch or sc.

Rnd 2: Ch 1, work in patt over next 0 (0, 1) sc; working around yarn floats, work in patt over next 8 (9, 9) chs, work in patt to end.

Upper Hand, Shape Top, Thumb

Work as for Right Mitten.

Finishing

With smaller hook, attach MC to lower edge of cuff at seam.

Rnd 1: Ch 1, work 32 (36, 40) sc evenly around, join with sl st to beg sc. Fasten off. Weave in ends.

Tie (make 2)

With MC and smaller hook, ch 101 (105, 109).

Row 1: Working through bottom bump of each ch, sl st in 2nd ch from hook and each ch across. Fasten off. Weave in ends.

Weave Ties in and out of the ch-1 sps from cuff. Tie in a bow to wear.

> **TIP:** Try adding pom-poms or tassels to the ends of the ties for added fun and interest!

Do the
Robot

Your guy is sure to crack a smile when you show off your crochet skills on these cute robot mitts. At first glance these robots are identical twins. But upon further examination, you'll find that they're each moving to the beat of their own robot music. And seriously, robots are pretty cool for chicks, too. Make yourself a pair!

FINISHED MEASUREMENTS
Palm Circumference: $7^3/_4$ ($8^1/_2$, $9^1/_2$)"/19.5 (21.5, 24) cm
Length: 8"/20.5 cm

SIZES
Men's Extra Small (Small, Medium)/Women's Small (Medium, Large)
Shown in Men's Small/Women's Medium.

YARN
Deborah Norville Collection Serenity Sock Solids by Premier Yarns, super fine weight #1 yarn (50% superwash merino wool, 25% bamboo, 25% nylon; 230 yds/1.75 oz; 210 m/50 g)
• 1 skein #DN150-12 Black (A)
• 1 skein #DN150-03 Red (B)

- 1 skein #DN150-11 Charcoal (C)
- 1 skein #DN150-08 Hot Lime (D)
- 1 skein #DN150-01 Soft White (E)

HOOK AND OTHER MATERIALS
- US B-1 (2.25 mm) crochet hook
- Tapestry needle
- Removable markers in 2 colors

GAUGE

28 sts x 28 rows in blo sc = 4"/10 cm square
Be sure to check your gauge!

NOTES
- The cuff is worked using the Fair Isle, or stranded, method of crochet. When changing colors in single crochet, work the first half of the stitch in the current color and then finish the stitch with the next color. See page 136 for a photo tutorial.
- See page 134 for a photo tutorial on tapestry crochet.
- For small areas of a color such as the red buttons on the front of the robot, work these stitches using a separate short length of yarn. Do not carry this color along throughout the entire round. Rather, keep this strand in the same place on the robot and only use it when you come to it in the round. This will keep the mitt from becoming too bulky.
- Instructions are given for placing removable markers. These markers are there to help keep track of both the Robot pattern and the thumb gusset. Consider using one color of marker for the thumb gusset and another color for the pattern as an additional helpful reminder.

Right Mitt

Note: Work each sc through the back loop only throughout the entire Mitt.

Cuff

With A, ch 48 (54, 60), join with sl st to beg ch, being careful not to twist.

Set-up rnd: Ch 1, sc in same st and in each ch around, join with sl st to beg sc—48 (54, 60) sc.

Rnd 1: Ch 1, sc in same sc, with B sc in next sc, [with A sc in next sc, with B sc in next sc] around, join with sl st to beg sc.

Rnds 2–15: Work Rnds 2–15 of Cuff Chart as established.

Rnd 16: With A, ch 1, sc in same sc and in each sc around, do not join.

Note: Remainder of Mitt is worked in a spiral.

Rnd 17: [2 sc in next sc, sc in next 7 (8, 9) sc] around—6 sts inc'd, 54 (60, 66) sc.

Hand

Note: Color A only is used for the hand except for in the areas of the Robot patt indicated by the chart.

Rnd 1: With A (and crocheting around C), sc in next 19 (21, 23) sts, place removable marker on st just worked (patt marker), work Row 1 of Right Hand Robot chart over 19 sc, with A sc in next sc, place removable marker on st just worked (patt marker), with A sc in rem 18 (20, 22) sc around.

Work 0 (1, 3) more rnd(s) in patt as established.

Thumb Gusset

Rnd 1: With A, sc in each sc through marked sc, work next row of Right Hand Robot chart over 19 sc, with A sc in next 4 (6, 8) sc, place removable marker on st just worked (Thumb marker), [2 sc in next sc] 2 times, sc in next sc, place removable marker on st just worked (Thumb marker), sc in last 9 (11, 13) sc—2 sts inc'd.

Rnd 2 (Inc rnd): With A, sc in each sc through patt marker, work next row of Right Hand Robot chart over 19 sc, with A sc in each sc through Thumb marker, 2 sc in next sc, sc in each sc to 1 sc before next Thumb marker, 2 sc in next sc, sc in each sc to end—2 sts inc'd.

Rep Inc rnd every rnd 3 more times, then rep Inc rnd every other rnd 5 (6, 7) times—20 (22, 24) Thumb sts inc'd, 64 (82, 90) sts total. The last Inc rnd worked will occur on Row 19 (19, 20) of Right Hand Robot chart.

Separate Thumb

Next rnd: With A, sc in each sc through patt marker, work Row 20 (20, 21) of Right Hand Robot chart over 19 sts, with A sc in next 5 (7, 9) sc, sk next 20 (22, 24) sc, sc in each sc to end—54 (60, 66) sts.

Cuff

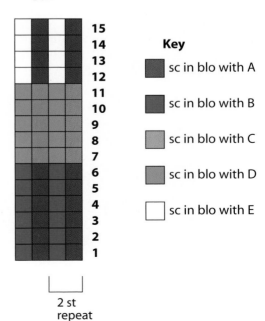

Key
- ■ sc in blo with A
- ■ sc in blo with B
- ▨ sc in blo with C
- ▨ sc in blo with D
- □ sc in blo with E

2 st
repeat

Robot Charts

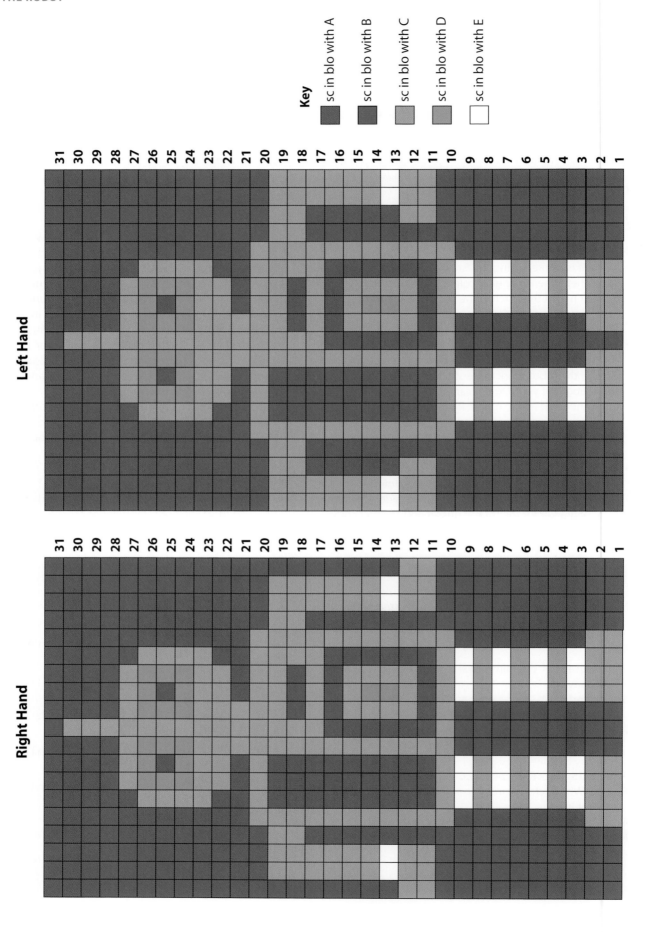

Left Hand

Right Hand

Key

sc in blo with A

sc in blo with B

sc in blo with C

sc in blo with D

sc in blo with E

Upper Hand

Cont in patt through Row 31 of Right Hand Robot chart. Cut all colors except A.

Next rnd: Sc in blo of each sc around.

Next rnd: Sc in blo of each sc around, join with sl st to beg sc.

Upper Edging

Note: Remainder of Hand is worked in joined rnds.

Rnd 1: Ch 1, with A, sc in same sc, with B sc in next sc, [with A sc in next sc, with B sc in next sc] around, join with sl st to beg sc.

Rnds 2–4: Rep Rnd 1.

Rnd 5: With A, ch 1, sc in blo of same sc and each sc around, join with sl st to beg sc. Fasten off.

Thumb

Attach A at center of Thumb gap.

Rnd 1: Ch 1, sc in same sp, sc in blo of next 20 (22, 24) sc, join with sl st to beg sc—21 (23, 25) sc.

Rnds 2–3: Ch 1, sc in blo of same sc and in each sc around, join with sl st to beg sc.

Fasten off.

Left Mitt

Cuff

Work as for Right Mitt, referencing Cuff Chart on page 73.

Hand

Note: Color A only is used for the hand except for in the areas of the Robot patt indicated by the chart.

Rnd 1: With A (and crocheting around C), sc in next 18 (20, 22) sts, place removable marker on st just worked (patt marker), work Row 1 of Left Hand Robot chart over 19 sc, with A sc in next sc, place removable marker on st just worked (patt marker), with A sc in rem 19 (21, 23) sc around.

Work 0 (1, 3) rnd(s) in patt as established.

Thumb Gusset

Rnd 1: With A, sc in next 10 (12, 14) sc, place removable marker on st just worked (Thumb marker), [2 sc in next sc] 2 times, sc in next sc, place removable marker on st just worked (Thumb marker), sc in each sc to patt marker, work next row of Left Hand Robot chart over 19 sc, with A sc in each sc to end—2 sts inc'd.

Rnd 2 (Inc rnd): With A, sc in each sc through Thumb marker, 2 sc in next sc, sc in each sc to 1 sc before next Thumb marker, 2 sc in next sc, sc in each sc to patt marker, work next row of Left Hand Robot chart over 19 sc, sc in each sc to end—2 sts inc'd.

Rep Inc rnd every rnd 3 times, then rep Inc rnd every other rnd 5 (6, 7) times—20 (22, 24) Thumb sts inc'd, 64 (82, 90) sts total. The last Inc rnd worked will occur on Row 19 (19, 20) of Left Hand Robot chart.

Separate Thumb

Next rnd: With A, sc in 1st 8 (10, 12) sc, sk next 20 (22, 24) sc, sc in each sc through patt marker, work Row 20 (20, 21) of Left Hand Robot chart over 19 sts, sc in each sc to end—54 (60, 66) sts.

Upper Hand, Upper Edging, Thumb

Work as for Right Mitt, referencing Left Hand Robot chart.

Finishing

Attach A to beg-ch edge. Sc in free lp of ch around, join with sl st to beg sc. Fasten off.

Weave in ends. Steam or wet block.

Upward Shift Mitts

T hese mitts are designed to play with self-shading and striping yarns. Make and assemble your strips as the colors appear in the ball, as shown. Or be adventurous! Join your strips in random order, or combine two self-shading yarns for a more complex look.

YARN

Universal Yarn Classic Shades, medium weight #4 yarn (70% acrylic, 30% wool; 197 yds/3.5 oz; 180 m/100 g)
• 1 ball #729 Lucky Rose

HOOKS AND OTHER MATERIALS

• US F-5 (3.75 mm) crochet hook
• US 7 (4.5 mm) crochet hook
• Tapestry needle

GAUGE

Using smaller hook, 15 sts x 18 rows in blo sc = 4"/10 cm square
Using larger hook, 16 sts x 19 rows in blo sc = 4"/10 cm square
Be sure to check your gauge!

NOTES

• These mitts are comprised of 7 (8, 9) strips. Each strip is worked widthwise, separately. The strips are joined by slip-stitching them together, leaving an opening for the thumb.

FINISHED MEASUREMENTS

Hand circumference: 7 (8, 9)"/18 (20.5, 23) cm
Length (not including leaf fringe): 6 (6^1/$_2$, 7)"/15 (16.5, 18) cm

SIZES

Women's Small (Medium, Large)
Shown in Women's Small.

Row 2 (WS): Ch 1, sc in blo of each sc across, turn.
Rows 3–10: Rep Row 2.
Switch to larger hook.
Rows 11–31 (11–33, 11–35): Rep Row 2.
Fasten off.

Right Mitt

Make 7 (8, 9) Strips.

Join Strips

Hold first and second Strips made with wrong sides facing
each other. Make a slipknot and place on smaller hook.
Beg at top (wider) edges, sl st Strips tog, working 1 sl st
into the side of each row. At the end of the Strips, [ch 4,
working through top loops of ch, work 3 hdc into 3rd ch
from hook, sl st in first ch of ch 4] (leaf fringe made).
Fasten off, leaving 4"/10 cm end. Use yarn end to secure
base of leaf fringe to inside of Mitt.
Hold second and third Strips with wrong sides facing each
other. Join Strips and make fringe as for previous 2
Strips. Join remaining Strips and make fringe in same
manner.

Final Seam/Thumb Opening

Hold first and last Strips with wrong sides facing each
other. Make a slipknot and place on smaller hook. Beg at
top edges, sl st Strips tog along first 9 rows, working
along last Strip only, sl st in side of next 11 (13, 15) rows,
working through both Strips again, sl st rem 11 rows
tog. At the end of the Strips, [ch 4, working through top
loops of ch, work 3 hdc into 3rd ch from hook, sl st in 1st
ch of ch 4] (leaf fringe made). Fasten off, leaving 4"/10
cm end. Use yarn end to secure base of leaf fringe to
inside of Mitt. Join yarn to unworked side of thumb
opening. Sl st along edge.

Left Mitt

Work as for Right Mitt. If matching mitts are desired, be sure
to begin at the same place in the color sequence of your
self-striping or self-shading yarn when beginning Strip
1. When joining Strips, work in reverse order so Right
and Left mitts are mirror images of one another,

Finishing

Top Edging
Join yarn to top edge of Mitt on palm. With smaller hook,
ch 1, work rev sc around, join with sl st to beg sc. Fasten
off.
Rep with other Mitt.
Weave in ends.

- Each strip begins by using a smaller hook. After 10 rows,
you will switch to a larger hook. By switching hook sizes,
each strip will be slightly wider at the top than at the
bottom. This will make for a snugger fit around both
hand and wrist.
- As shown, the first strip of each mitt begins at
approximately the same place in the shading scheme.
The first strip is fastened off and each successive strip is
begun from the point in the ball where the previous strip
left off. The bright pink color in the slip-stitch seams and
top edging is one of the colors in the yarn that was
reserved for the trim.

STITCH GUIDE
Reverse Single Crochet (rev sc)
Working from left to right, sc in each st around.

STITCH PATTERN
Strip
With smaller hook, ch 5.
Row 1 (RS): Sc in blo of 2nd ch from hook and in blo of
each ch across, turn—4 sc.

Hi-Lo

Inspired by the unbalanced hems of shirts and skirts popular in the fashion world and in ready-to-wear items, Hi-Lo mitts are fashion-forward, for sure. They're a little bit peek-a-boo on top of the arm and hand and provide a bit more coverage underneath. Walk down the street in style in these babies!

FINISHED MEASUREMENTS
Forearm: 9 (10, 11)"/23 (25.5, 28) cm
Hand circumference: 7 (8, 9)"/18 (20.5, 23) cm
Length: 11 (11^1/$_2$, 12^1/$_4$)"/28 (29, 31) cm

SIZES
Women's Small (Medium, Large)
Shown in Small.

YARN

Deborah Norville Collection Serenity Garden by Premier Yarns, fine weight #2 yarn (100% dralon microfiber; 185 yds/2.29 oz; 169 m/65 g)
• 2 balls #800-07 Crocus

HOOKS AND OTHER MATERIALS

• US E-4 (3.5 mm) crochet hook
• US C-2 (2.75 mm) crochet hook
• US B-1 (2.25 mm) crochet hook
• Tapestry needle

GAUGE

Using largest hook, 20 sts x 16 rows in blo sc = 4"/10 cm square
Using medium hook, 24 sts x 19 rows in blo sc = 4"/10 cm square
Be sure to check your gauge!

NOTES

• These long mitts are worked from the cuff up. Shaping is achieved by changing hook size. The work begins with the largest hook for the forearm, shifts down to the smallest hook at the wrist, and continues with the medium hook for the remainder of the hand. This assures a snug fit around all portions of the arm and hand.
• The arm is worked in joined rows; the thumb opening section rows are not joined. Work resumes in joined rows above the thumb opening.
• If you're using a self-striping or shading yarn such as Serenity Garden (shown), be sure to start each mitt at the same place in the color repeat to ensure a matching pair.

STITCH GUIDE

Spike Slip Stitch (spike sl st)
Insert hook in sp or st indicated from front to back, pull through lp (2 lps on hook), bring lp about three quarters of the way even with the current row (slightly gathering the work) and through first lp on hook.

Right Mitt

Arm

With largest hook, ch 59 (67, 75). Join with sl st through bottom bump of first ch to form ring.

Set-up row (RS): Working through bottom bump of each ch, ch 1, sc2tog in same st and next ch, sc in next 4 (5, 6) chs, 3 sc in next ch, sc in next 4 (5, 6) chs, sc2tog, [sc2tog, sc in next 4 (5, 6) chs, 3 sc in next ch, sc in next 4 (5, 6) chs, sc2tog] 2 times, sc2tog, sc in next ch, 3 sc in next ch, sc in next ch, [sc2tog] 2 times, sc in next 4 (5, 6) chs, 3 sc in next ch, sc in next 4 (5, 6) chs, sc2tog, join with sl st to beg sc, turn—59 (67, 75) sc.
Note: Work through blo of each sc unless otherwise noted.

Row 1 (WS): Ch 1, sc2tog, sc in next 4 (5, 6) sc, 3 sc in next sc, sc in next 4 (5, 6) sc, [sc2tog] 2 times, sc in next sc, 3 sc

in next sc, sc in next sc, sc2tog, [sc2tog, sc in next 4 (5, 6) sc, 3 sc in next sc, sc in next 4 (5, 6) sc, sc2tog] 3 times, join with sl st to beg sc, turn.

Row 2: Ch 1, [sc2tog, sc in next 4 (5, 6) sc, 3 sc in next sc, sc in next 4 (5, 6) sc, sc2tog] 3 times, sc2tog, sc in next sc, 3 sc in next sc, sc in next sc, [sc2tog] 2 times, sc in next 4 (5, 6) sc, 3 sc in next sc, sc in next 4 (5, 6) sc, sc2tog, join with sl st to beg sc, turn.

Row 3: Rep Row 1.

Row 4: Ch 1, [sc2tog, sc in next 4 (5, 6) sc, 3 sc in next sc, sc in next 4 (5, 6) sc, sc2tog] 3 times, spike sl st between sc2togs from 4 rows below, sc2tog, sc in next sc, 3 sc in next sc, sc in next sc, sc2tog, spike sl st between sc2togs from 4 rows below, sc2tog, sc in next 4 (5, 6) sc, 3 sc in next sc, sc in next 4 (5, 6) sc, sc2tog, join with sl st to beg sc, turn.

Row 5: Ch 1, sc2tog, sc in next 4 (5, 6) sc, 3 sc in next sc, sc in next 4 (5, 6) sc, sc2tog, skip spike sl st, sc2tog, sc in next sc, 3 sc in next sc, sc in next sc, sc2tog, skip spike sl st, [sc2tog, sc in next 4 (5, 6) sc, 3 sc in next sc, sc in next 4 (5, 6) sc, sc2tog] 3 times, join with sl st to beg sc, turn.

Rows 6–7: Rep Rows 2–3.

Row 8: Ch 1, [sc2tog, sc in next 4 (5, 6) sc, 3 sc in next sc, sc in next 4 (5, 6) sc, sc2tog] 3 times, spike sl st through center of previous spike sl st, sc2tog, sc in next sc, 3 sc in next sc, sc in next sc, sc2tog, spike sl st through center of previous spike sl st, sc2tog, sc in next 4 (5, 6) sc, 3 sc in next sc, sc in next 4 (5, 6) sc, sc2tog, join with sl st to beg sc, turn.

Rows 9–12: Rep Rows 5–8. There are now 3 levels of spike sl sts.

Switch to medium hook.

Rows 13–24: [Rep Rows 5–8] 3 times. There are now 6 levels of spike sl sts.

Switch to smallest hook.

Rows 25–28: Rep Rows 5–8. There are now 7 levels of spike sl sts.

Switch back to medium hook.

Rows 29–32: Rep Rows 5–8. There are now 8 levels of spike sl sts.

Thumb Opening

Note: Mitt continues in pattern as established. The only difference is that the rows are not joined.

Row 1 (WS): Ch 1, sc2tog, sc in next 4 (5, 6) sc, 3 sc in next sc, sc in next 4 (5, 6) sc, sc2tog, skip spike sl st, sc2tog, sc in next sc, 3 sc in next sc, sc in next sc, sc2tog, skip spike sl st, [sc2tog, sc in next 4 (5, 6) sc, 3 sc in next sc, sc in next 4 (5, 6) sc, sc2tog] 3 times, turn.

Row 2 (RS): Ch 1, [sc2tog, sc in next 4 (5, 6) sc, 3 sc in next sc, sc in next 4 (5, 6) sc, sc2tog] 3 times, sc2tog, sc in next sc, 3 sc in next sc, sc in next sc, [sc2tog] 2 times, sc in next 4 (5, 6) sc, 3 sc in next sc, sc in next 4 (5, 6) sc, sc2tog, turn.

Row 3: Ch 1, sc2tog, sc in next 4 (5, 6) sc, 3 sc in next sc, sc in next 4 (5, 6) sc, [sc2tog] 2 times, sc in next sc, 3 sc in next sc, sc in next sc, sc2tog, [sc2tog, sc in next 4 (5, 6) sc, 3 sc in next sc, sc in next 4 (5, 6) sc, sc2tog] 3 times, turn.

Row 4: Ch 1, [sc2tog, sc in next 4 (5, 6) sc, 3 sc in next sc, sc in next 4 (5, 6) sc, sc2tog] 3 times, spike sl st through center of previous spike sl st, sc2tog, sc in next sc, 3 sc in next sc, sc in next sc, sc2tog, spike sl st through center of previous spike sl st, sc2tog, sc in next 4 (5, 6) sc, 3 sc in next sc, sc in next 4 (5, 6) sc, sc2tog, turn.

Rows 5–12 (5–12, 5–16): [Rep Rows 1–4] 2 (2, 3) times. There are now 11 (11, 12) levels of spike sl sts.

Medium Size Only

Rows 13–14: Rep Rows 1–2.

Rejoin Hand.

Rep Rows 1 and 8 of Arm Section. There are now 12 levels of spike sl sts.

All Sizes

Rejoin Hand (Medium size is already rejoined).

Rep Rows 5–8 of Arm section 2 (2, 3) times. There are now 13 (14, 15) levels of spike sl sts. Fasten off.

Left Mitt

Arm

With largest hook, ch 59 (67, 75). Join with sl st through bottom bump of 1st ch to form ring.

Set-up row (RS): Working through bottom bump of each ch, ch 1, sc2tog in same st and next ch, sc in next 4 (5, 6) chs, 3 sc in next ch, sc in next 4 (5, 6) chs, [sc2tog] 2 times, sc in next ch, 3 sc in next ch, sc in next ch, sc2tog, [sc2tog, sc in next 4 (5, 6) chs, 3 sc in next ch, sc in next 4 (5, 6) chs, sc2tog] 3 times, join with sl st to beg sc, turn.

Note: Work through blo of each sc unless otherwise noted.

Row 1 (WS): Ch 1, [sc2tog, sc in next 4 (5, 6) sc, 3 sc in next sc, sc in next 4 (5, 6) sc, sc2tog] 3 times, sc2tog, sc in next sc, 3 sc in next sc, sc in next sc, [sc2tog] 2 times, sc in next 4 (5, 6) sc, 3 sc in next sc, sc in next 4 (5, 6) sc, sc2tog, join with sl st to beg sc, turn.

Row 2: Ch 1, sc2tog, sc in next 4 (5, 6) sc, 3 sc in next sc, sc in next 4 (5, 6) sc, [sc2tog] 2 times, sc in next sc, 3 sc in next sc, sc in next sc, sc2tog, [sc2tog, sc in next 4 (5, 6) sc, 3 sc in next sc, sc in next 4 (5, 6) sc, sc2tog] 3 times, join with sl st to beg sc, turn.

Row 3: Rep Row 1.

Row 4: Ch 1, sc2tog, sc in next 4 (5, 6) sc, 3 sc in next sc, sc in next 4 (5, 6) sc, sc2tog, spike sl st between sc2togs from 4 rows below, sc2tog, sc in next sc, 3 sc in next sc, sc in next sc, sc2tog, spike sl st between sc2togs from 4 rows below [sc2tog, sc in next 4 (5, 6) sc, 3 sc in next sc, sc in next 4 (5, 6) sc, sc2tog] 3 times, join with sl st to beg sc, turn.

Row 5: Ch 1, [sc2tog, sc in next 4 (5, 6) sc, 3 sc in next sc, sc in next 4 (5, 6) sc, sc2tog] 3 times, skip spike sl st, sc2tog, sc in next sc, 3 sc in next sc, sc in next sc, sc2tog, skip spike sl st, sc2tog, sc in next 4 (5, 6) sc, 3 sc in next sc, sc in next 4 (5, 6) sc, sc2tog, join with sl st to beg sc, turn.

Rows 6–7: Rep Rows 2–3.

Row 8: Ch 1, sc2tog, sc in next 4 (5, 6) sc, 3 sc in next sc, sc in next 4 (5, 6) sc, sc2tog, spike sl st through center of

previous spike sl st, sc2tog, sc in next sc, 3 sc in next sc, sc in next sc, sc2tog, spike sl st through center of previous spike sl st [sc2tog, sc in next 4 (5, 6) sc, 3 sc in next sc, sc in next 4 (5, 6) sc, sc2tog] 3 times, join with sl st to beg sc, turn.

Rows 9–12: Rep Rows 5–8. There are now 3 levels of spike sl sts.

Switch to medium hook.

Rows 13–24: [Rep Rows 5–8] 3 times. There are now 6 levels of spike sl sts.

Switch to smallest hook.

Rows 25–28: Rep Rows 5–8. There are now 7 levels of spike sl sts.

Switch back to medium hook.

Rows 29–32: Rep Rows 5–8. There are now 8 levels of spike sl sts.

Thumb Opening

Note: Mitt continues in pattern as established. The only difference is that the rows are not joined.

Row 1 (WS): Ch 1, [sc2tog, sc in next 4 (5, 6) sc, 3 sc in next sc, sc in next 4 (5, 6) sc, sc2tog] 3 times, skip spike sl st, sc2tog, sc in next sc, 3 sc in next sc, sc in next sc, sc2tog, skip spike sl st, sc2tog, sc in next 4 (5, 6) sc, 3 sc in next sc, sc in next 4 (5, 6) sc, sc2tog, turn.

Row 2 (RS): Ch 1, sc2tog, sc in next 4 (5, 6) sc, 3 sc in next sc, sc in next 4 (5, 6) sc, [sc2tog] 2 times, sc in next sc, 3 sc in next sc, sc in next sc, sc2tog, [sc2tog, sc in next 4 (5, 6) sc, 3 sc in next sc, sc in next 4 (5, 6) sc, sc2tog] 3 times, turn.

Row 3: Ch 1, [sc2tog, sc in next 4 (5, 6) sc, 3 sc in next sc, sc in next 4 (5, 6) sc, sc2tog] 3 times, sc2tog, sc in next sc, 3 sc in next sc, sc in next sc, [sc2tog] 2 times, sc in next 4 (5, 6) sc, 3 sc in next sc, sc in next 4 (5, 6) sc, sc2tog, turn.

Row 4: Ch 1, sc2tog, sc in next 4 (5, 6) sc, 3 sc in next sc, sc in next 4 (5, 6) sc, sc2tog, spike sl st through center of previous spike sl st, sc2tog, sc in next sc, 3 sc in next sc, sc in next sc, sc2tog, spike sl st through center of previous spike sl st [sc2tog, sc in next 4 (5, 6) sc, 3 sc in next sc, sc in next 4 (5, 6) sc, sc2tog] 3 times, turn.

Rows 5–12 (5–12, 5–16): [Rep Rows 1–4] 2 (2, 3) times. There are now 11 (11, 12) levels of spike sl sts.

Medium Size Only

Rows 13–14: Rep Rows 1–2.

Rejoin Hand.

Rep Rows 1 and 8 of Arm Section. There are now 12 levels of spike sl sts.

All Sizes

Rejoin Hand (Medium size is already rejoined).

Rep Rows 5–8 of Arm section 2 (2, 3) times. There are now 13 (14, 15) levels of spike sl sts. Fasten off.

Finishing

Weave in ends.

Moto
Mitts

Put a little bit of tough into your next crochet project with these sassy mitts. You can go glam meets biker girl as shown, with metallic purple yarn and black beads, be an angel in disguise with an all-white pair, or come up with something totally different!

FINISHED MEASUREMENTS
Palm circumference: $7^1/2$ ($8^1/2$, $9^1/4$)"/19 (21.5, 23.5) cm
Length: 6 ($6^1/2$, 7)"/15 (16.5, 18) cm

SIZES
Women's Small (Medium, Large)
Shown in Small.

YARN
Nazli Gelin Garden 10 Metallic, lace weight #0 yarn (99% mercerized Egyptian Giza cotton, 1% metallic; 308 yds/1.75 oz; 282 m/50 g)
• 1 ball #11 Purple with Silver Metallic

HOOK AND OTHER MATERIALS
• US steel 7 (1.65 mm) crochet hook
• 66 (78, 90) 10/0 black glass seed beeds
• Tapestry needle
• Removable stitch markers
• Two $^5/8$"/1.5 cm shank buttons
• Two $^3/8$"/1 cm sew-on snap fastener sets
• Sewing needle and thread

GAUGE
40 sts x 34 rows in blo sc = 4"/10 cm square
Be sure to check your gauge!

NOTES
• These gloves are worked from the top down. Fingers and thumb are made first and then joined to work in the round.

STITCH GUIDE
Foundation Single Crochet (fsc)
Place a slip knot on the hook. Ch 2. Insert hook into second ch from hook, yo, pull yo through ch (2 lps on hook), yo and pull through first lp on hook (2 lps on hook), yo and pull

through both lps—first foundation sc made. *Insert hook under 2 lps of ch portion from previous foundation sc, yo and pull through (2 lps on hook), yo and pull through first lp on hook (2 lps on hook), yo and pull through both lps—foundation sc made; rep from * for as many sc as required.

Single Crochet with Bead (sc-b)

Slide bead up close to hook, holding bead with your left hand and keeping it at the front of the work. Going behind the bead, insert hook into st indicated, pull up a lp, yo, and pull through both lps, keeping bead at front of work.

Right Mitt

Thumb

Fsc 26 (28, 30), join with sl st to form ring.

Rnd 1: Ch 1, sc in same sc, sc in each sc around, do not join—26 (28, 30) sc.

Rnds 2–6: Sc in blo of each sc around. Fasten off, leaving a 4"/10 cm tail for closing any gaps left between fingers. Weave in tail from beg ch.

Pinky Finger

Fsc 22 (24, 26), join with sl st to form ring.

Rnd 1: Ch 1, sc in same sc, sc in each sc around, do not join—22 (24, 26) sc.

Rnds 2–6: Sc in blo of each sc around. Fasten off, leaving a 4"/10 cm tail for closing any gaps left between fingers. Weave in tail from beg ch.

Ring Finger

Fsc 24 (26, 28), join with sl st to form ring.

Rnd 1: Ch 1, sc in same sc, sc in each sc around, do not join—24 (26, 28) sc.

Rnds 2–6: Sc in blo of each sc around. Fasten off, leaving a 4"/10 cm tail for closing any gaps left between fingers. Weave in tail from beg ch.

Middle Finger

Work as for Ring Finger.

String 66 (78, 90) beads onto yarn before beginning Index Finger.

Index Finger

Work as for Ring Finger, but do not fasten off.

Join Fingers

Note: Work all sc through blo unless otherwise noted.

Rnd 1: Sc2tog (next 2 sts from Index Finger), working across Middle Finger, sc2tog, sc in next 8 (9, 10) sc, sc2tog, working across Ring Finger, sc2tog, sc in next 8 (9, 10) sc, sc2tog, working across Pinky Finger, sc2tog, sc in next 18 (20, 24) sc, sc2tog, working across Ring Finger, sc2tog, sc in next 8 (9, 10) sc, sc2tog, working across Middle Finger, sc2tog, sc in next 8 (9, 10) sc, sc2tog,

working across Index Finger, sc2tog, sc in next 20 (22, 24) sc, do not join—82 (90, 98) sc.

Rnd 2: Sc2tog (next sc from index finger tog with next sc from middle finger), sc in next 8 (9, 10) sc, sc2tog (next sc from middle finger tog with next sc from ring finger), sc in next 8 (9, 10) sc, sc2tog (next sc from ring finger tog with next sc from pinky finger), sc in next 18 (20, 22) sc, sc2tog, sc in next 8 (9, 10) sc, sc2tog, sc in next 8 (9, 10) sc, sc2tog, sc in next 66 (73, 80) sc—76 (84, 92) sc. You should now be between the middle and ring fingers, with the pinky to your right and index finger to the left. Place a removable marker on the next st to indicate beg of rnd.

Note: Work continues in a spiral, do not join rounds.

Rnds 3–4: Sc in each sc around.

Establish Pattern

Rnd 1: Sc in next 29 (32, 35) sc (the next sc should be one sc before the space between the index and middle fingers), [sc-b in next sc, fpdc around post of sc from 2 rows below, sk sc behind fpdc just made, sc-b in next sc, sc in next 6 (7, 8) sc] 2 times, sc-b in next sc, fpdc around post of sc from 2 rows below, sk sc behind fpdc just made, sc-b in next sc, sc in each rem sc around.

Rnd 2: Sc in each st around.

Rnd 3: Sc in next 29 (32, 35) sc, [sc-b in next sc, fpdc around post of dc from 2 rows below, sk sc behind fpdc just made, sc-b in next sc, sc in next 6 (7, 8) sc] 2 times, sc-b in next sc, fpdc around post of dc from 2 rows below, sk sc behind fpdc just made, sc-b in next sc, sc in each rem sc around.

Rnd 4: Sc in each st around.

The sc-b and fpdc sts from Rnd 3 and plain sc from Rnd 4 form patt.

[Rep Rnds 3–4] 4 (5, 6) more times—36 (42, 48) beads have been placed.

Thumb Gusset, Shape Top of Hand

Rnd 1: Sc in next 21 (23, 25) sc, place removable marker on last sc just worked (move this marker up each rnd), sc2tog (next sc tog with Thumb st), sc in next 24 (26, 28) Thumb sts, sc2tog (last Thumb st tog with next st from Hand), sc in next sc, place removable marker on last sc just worked (move this marker up each rnd), sc in next 6 (7, 8) sc, [sc-b in next sc, fpdc around post of dc from 2 rows below, sk sc behind fpdc just made, sc-b in next sc, sc2tog, sc in next 4 (5, 6) sc] 2 times, sc-b in next sc, fpdc around post of dc from 2 rows below, sk sc behind fpdc just made, sc-b in next sc, sc in each rem sc around—98 (108, 118) sts; 2 Thumb sts dec'd, 2 sts on top of Hand between beaded lines dec'd.

Rnd 2: Sc in each st around.

Rnd 3: Sc in each sc through marked sc, sc2tog, sc in each sc to 2 sc before next marked sc, sc2tog, sc in next 6 (7, 8) sc, [sc-b in next sc, fpdc around post of dc from 2 rows below, sk sc behind fpdc just made, sc-b in next sc, sc in next 5 (6, 7) sc] 2 times, sc-b in next sc, fpdc around post of dc from 2 rows below, sk sc behind fpdc just made, sc-b in next sc, sc in each rem sc around—96 (106, 116) sts; 2 Thumb sts dec'd.

Rnd 4: Sc in each st around.

Rnd 5: Sc in each sc through marked sc, sc2tog, sc in each sc to 2 sc before next marked sc, sc2tog, sc in next 6 (7, 8) sc, [sc-b in next sc, fpdc around post of dc from 2 rows below, sk sc behind fpdc just made, sc-b in next sc, sc in next 3 (4, 5) sc, sc2tog] 2 times, sc-b in next sc, fpdc around post of dc from 2 rows below, sk sc behind fpdc just made, sc-b in next sc, sc in each rem sc around—92 (102, 112) sts; 2 Thumb sts dec'd, 2 sts on top of Hand between beaded lines dec'd.

Rnd 6: Sc in each st around.

Rnd 7: Sc in each sc through marked sc, sc2tog, sc in each sc to 2 sc before next marked sc, sc2tog, sc in next 6 (7, 8) sc, [sc-b in next sc, fpdc around post of dc from 2 rows below, sk sc behind fpdc just made, sc-b in next sc, sc in next 4 (5, 6) sc] 2 times, sc-b in next sc, fpdc around post of dc from 2 rows below, sk sc behind fpdc just made, sc-b in next sc, sc in each rem sc around—90 (100, 110) sts rem; 2 Thumb sts dec'd.

Rnd 8: Sc in each st around.

Rnd 9: Sc in each sc through marked sc, sc2tog, sc in each sc to 2 sc before next marked sc, sc2tog, sc in next 6 (7, 8) sc, [sc-b in next sc, fpdc around post of dc from 2 rows below, sk sc behind fpdc just made, sc-b in next sc, sc2tog, sc in next 2 (3, 4) sc] 2 times, sc-b in next sc, fpdc around post of dc from 2 rows below, sk sc behind fpdc just made, sc-b in next sc, sc in each rem sc around—86 (96, 106) sts; 2 Thumb sts dec'd, 2 sts on top of Hand between beaded lines dec'd.

Medium & Large Sizes Only

Rnd 10: Sc in each st around.

Rnd 11: Sc in each sc through marked sc, sc2tog, sc in each sc to 2 sc before next marked sc, sc2tog, sc in next 7 (8) sc, [sc-b in next sc, fpdc around post of dc from 2 rows below, sk sc behind fpdc just made, sc-b in next sc, sc in next 2 (3) sc, sc2tog] 2 times, sc-b in next sc, fpdc around post of dc from 2 rows below, sk sc behind fpdc just made, sc-b in next sc, sc in each rem sc around—92 (102) sts; 2 Thumb sts dec'd, 2 sts on top of Hand between beaded lines dec'd.

Large Size Only

Rnd 12: Sc in each st around.

Rnd 13: Sc in each sc through marked sc, sc2tog, sc in each sc to 2 sc before next marked sc, sc2tog, sc in next 8 sc, [sc-b in next sc, fpdc around post of dc from 2 rows below, sk sc behind fpdc just made, sc-b in next sc, sc in next 2 sc, sc2tog] 2 times, sc-b in next sc, fpdc around post of dc from 2 rows below, sk sc behind fpdc just made, sc-b in next sc, sc in each rem sc around—98 sts; 2 Thumb sts dec'd, 2 sts on top of Hand between beaded lines dec'd.

Keyhole Opening, Continue to Work Thumb Gusset

Note: Remainder of Mitt is worked back and forth in rows.

Row 1 (RS): Sc in each sc through the last sc before the first sc-b, turn.

Row 2 (WS): Ch 1, sl st in blo of next 71 (77, 83) sc (ending just before center 15 sts), turn.

Note: Work all scs on RS rows through back (unworked) lp of sc from 2 rows previous.

Row 3: Ch 1, sc in blo of sc from 2 rows previous, sc2tog, sc in each sc to marked sc, sc2tog, sc in each sc through marked sc, sc2tog, sc in each sc to last 3 sc, sc2tog, sc in last sc, turn—67 (73, 79) sts; 2 Thumb sts dec'd, 2 sts dec'd at Keyhole opening.

Row 4: Ch 1, sl st in blo of each sc across, turn.

Rows 5–10: [Rep Rows 3–4] 3 more times—55 (61, 67) sts.

Row 11: Ch 1, sc in blo of sc from 2 rows previous, sc in each sc to marked st, sc2tog, sc in each sc through marked sc, sc2tog, sc in each sc to end—53 (59, 65) sts.

Row 12: Ch 1, sl st in blo of each sc across, turn.

Rows 13–16: [Rep Rows 11–12] 2 times—49 (55, 61) sts.

Wristband

Row 1 (RS): Sl st in blo of sc from 2 rows previous, ch 3 (counts as dc), dc in blo of each sc from 2 rows previous across, ch 19 for Wristband, turn.

Row 2 (WS): Ch 1, sl st in blo of 2nd ch from hook and next 17 chs, sl st in blo of each sc across, ch 6 for Wrist Tab, turn.

Note: Work all scs on RS rows through back (unworked) lp of sc or dc from 2 rows previous.

Row 3: Sc through back lp and bottom bump of second ch from hook and next 4 chs, sc in next 49 (55, 61) dc, sc in blo of last 18 sts of free (unworked) ch from 2 rows previous, turn—72 (78, 84) sc.

Row 4: Ch 1, sl st in blo of each sc across, turn.

Row 5: Ch 1, sc in blo of 1st sc, sc in each sc to last 2 sc, 2 sc in next sc, sc in last sc—73 (79, 85) sc.

Row 6: Ch 1, sl st in blo of each sc across, turn.

Rows 7–8: Rep Rows 5–6—74 (80, 86) sc.

Row 9: Ch 1, sc in blo of 1st sc, sc in each sc to end, turn.

Row 10: Ch 1, sl st in blo of each sc across, turn.

Row 11: Sl st in blo of sc from 2 rows previous, ch 3 (counts as dc), dc in blo of each sc from 2 rows previous across, turn.

Row 12: Ch 1, sl st in blo of each sc across, turn.

Row 13: Ch 1, sc in blo of 1st dc from 2 rows previous, sc in each dc to end, turn.

Row 14: Ch 1, sl st in blo of each sc across, turn.

Row 15: Ch 1, sc in blo of 1st sc, sc in each sc to last 3 sc, sc2tog, sc in last sc, turn—72 (78, 84) sc.

Row 16: Ch 1, sl st in blo of each sc across, turn.

Row 17: Rep Row 15, do not turn—71 (77, 83) sc.

Keyhole Edging

Rotate work 90 degrees clockwise.

Row 1 (RS): Working along the side of Wristband, ch 1, work 10 sc evenly along side of Tab, 3 sc in corner, work 18 sc along edge of Wristband; working at the rate of 1 sc for every other sc/sl st row, 2 sc for every dc, and 1 sc for every sc, sc evenly around Keyhole opening; working along beg-ch edge of top of Wrist Tab, sc through free lp of beg ch of next 5 sts, work 3 sc in corner, work 10 sc evenly along side of Wristband, 2 sc in corner, join with sl st to beg sc from Row 17, turn.

Row 2 (WS): Sl st in blo of each sc along side of Wrist Tab, along top edge, around Keyhole opening, along top edge of Wristband, side of Wristband, and along bottom edge of Row 17 of Cuff, join with sl st to beg sl st, fasten off.

Left Mitt

Thumb, Pinky, Ring, Middle, and Index Fingers
Work as for Right Mitt.

Join Fingers

Note: Work all sc through blo unless otherwise noted.

Rnd 1: Sc2tog (next 2 sts from Index Finger), working across Middle Finger, sc2tog, sc in next 8 (9, 10) sc, sc2tog, working across Ring Finger, sc2tog, sc in next 8 (9, 10) sc, sc2tog, working across Pinky Finger, sc2tog, sc in next 18 (20, 24) sc, sc2tog, working across Ring Finger, sc2tog, sc in next 8 (9, 10) sc, sc2tog, working across Middle Finger, sc2tog, sc in next 8 (9, 10) sc, sc2tog, working across Index Finger, sc2tog, sc in next 20 (22, 24) sc, do not join—82 (90, 98) sc.

Note: The remainder of the mitt is worked in a spiral. Do not join rounds.

Rnd 2: Sc2tog (next sc from index finger tog with next sc from middle finger), sc in next 8 (9, 10) sc, sc2tog (next sc from middle finger tog with next sc from ring finger), sc in next 8 (9, 10) sc, sc2tog (next sc from ring finger tog with next sc from pinky finger), sc in next 18 (20, 22) sc, sc2tog, sc in next 8 (9, 10) sc, sc2tog, sc in next 8 (9, 10) sc, sc2tog, sc in next 29 (33, 37) sc—76 (84, 92) sc. You should now be between the middle and ring fingers with the index finger to your right and pinky to your left. This is the beg of rnd. Place a removable marker on the next st to indicate beg of rnd.

Rnds 3–4: Sc in each sc around.

Establish Pattern

Rnd 1: Sc in next 27 (30, 33) sc (the next sc should be one sc before the space between the pinky and ring fingers), [sc-b in next sc, fpdc around post of sc from 2 rows below, sk sc behind fpdc just made, sc-b in next sc, sc in next 6 (7, 8) sc] 2 times, sc-b in next sc, fpdc around post of sc from 2 rows below, sk sc behind fpdc just made, sc-b in next sc, sc in each rem sc around.

Rnd 2: Sc in each st around.

Rnd 3: Sc in next 27 (30, 33) sc, [sc-b in next sc, fpdc around post of dc from 2 rows below, sk sc behind fpdc just made, sc-b in next sc, sc in next 6 (7, 8) sc] twice, sc-b in next sc, fpdc around post of dc from 2 rows below, sk sc behind fpdc just made, sc-b in next sc, sc in each rem sc around.

Rnd 4: Sc in each st around.

The sc-b and fpdc sts from Rnd 3 and plain sc from Rnd 4 form patt.

[Rep Rnds 3–4] 4 (5, 6) more times; 36 (42, 48) beads have been placed.

Thumb Gusset, Shape Top of Hand

Rnd 1: Sc in next 27 (30, 33) sc, [sc-b in next sc, fpdc around post of dc from 2 rows below, sk sc behind fpdc just made, sc-b in next sc, sc2tog, sc in next 4 (5, 6) sc] 2 times, sc-b in next sc, fpdc around post of dc from 2 rows below, sk sc behind fpdc just made, sc-b in next sc, sc in next 7 (8, 9) sc, place removable marker on last sc just worked (move this marker up each rnd) sc2tog (next sc tog with Thumb st), sc in next 24 (26, 28) Thumb sts,

sc2tog (last Thumb st tog with next st from Hand), sc in next sc, place removable marker on last sc just worked (move this marker up each rnd) sc in each rem sc around—98 (108, 118) sts; 2 Thumb sts dec'd, 2 sts on top of Hand between beaded lines dec'd.

Rnd 2: Sc in each st around.

Rnd 3: Sc in next 27 (30, 33) sc, [sc-b in next sc, fpdc around post of dc from 2 rows below, sk sc behind fpdc just made, sc-b in next sc, sc in next 5 (6, 7) sc] twice, sc-b in next sc, fpdc around post of dc from 2 rows below, sk sc behind fpdc just made, sc-b in next sc, sc in each sc through marked sc, sc2tog, sc in each sc to 2 sc before next marked sc, sc2tog, sc in each rem sc around—96 (106, 116) sts; 2 Thumb sts dec'd.

Rnd 4: Sc in each st around.

Rnd 5: Sc in next 27 (30, 33) sc, [sc-b in next sc, fpdc around post of dc from 2 rows below, sk sc behind fpdc just made, sc-b in next sc, sc in next 3 (4, 5) sc, sc2tog] 2 times, sc-b in next sc, fpdc around post of dc from 2 rows below, sk sc behind fpdc just made, sc-b in next sc, sc in each sc through marked sc, sc2tog, sc in each sc to 2 sc before next marked sc, sc2tog, sc in each rem sc around—92 (102, 112) sts; 2 Thumb sts dec'd, 2 sts on top of Hand dec'd.

Rnd 6: Sc in each st around.

Rnd 7: Sc in next 27 (30, 33) sc, [sc-b in next sc, fpdc around post of dc from 2 rows below, sk sc behind fpdc just made, sc-b in next sc, sc in next 4 (5, 6) sc] 2 times, sc-b in next sc, fpdc around post of dc from 2 rows below, sk sc behind fpdc just made, sc-b in next sc, sc in each sc through marked sc, sc2tog, sc in each sc to 2 sc before next marked sc, sc2tog, sc in each rem sc around—90 (100, 110) sts; 2 Thumb sts dec'd.

Rnd 8: Sc in each st around.

Rnd 9: Sc in next 27 (30, 33) sc, [sc-b in next sc, fpdc around post of dc from 2 rows below, sk sc behind fpdc just made, sc-b in next sc, sc2tog, sc in next 2 (3, 4) sc] 2 times, sc-b in next sc, fpdc around post of dc from 2 rows below, sk sc behind fpdc just made, sc-b in next sc, sc in each sc through marked sc, sc2tog, sc in each sc to 2 sc before next marked sc, sc2tog, sc in each rem sc around—86 (96, 106) sts; 2 Thumb sts dec'd, 2 sts on top of Hand dec'd.

Medium & Large Sizes Only

Rnd 10: Sc in each st around.

Rnd 11: Sc in next 30 (33) sc, [sc-b in next sc, fpdc around post of dc from 2 rows below, sk sc behind fpdc just made, sc-b in next sc, sc in next 2 (3) sc, sc2tog] 2 times, sc-b in next sc, fpdc around post of dc from 2 rows below, sk sc behind fpdc just made, sc-b in next sc, sc in each sc through marked sc, sc2tog, sc in each sc to 2 sc before next marked sc, sc2tog, sc in each rem sc around—92 (102) sts; 2 Thumb sts dec'd, 2 sts on top of Hand dec'd.

Large Size Only

Rnd 12: Sc in each st around.

Rnd 13: Sc in next 33 sc, [sc-b in next sc, fpdc around post of dc from 2 rows below, sk sc behind fpdc just made, sc-b in next sc, sc in next 2 sc, sc2tog] 2 times, sc-b in next sc, fpdc around post of dc from 2 rows below, sk sc behind fpdc just made, sc-b in next sc, sc in each sc through marked sc, sc2tog, sc in each sc to 2 sc before next marked sc, sc2tog, sc in each rem sc around—98 sts; 2 Thumb sts dec'd, 2 sts on top of Hand dec'd.

Keyhole Opening, Continue to Work Thumb Gusset

Note: Remainder of Mitt is worked back and forth in rows.

Row 1 (RS): Sc in each of next 27 (30, 33) sc, turn.

Row 2 (WS): Ch 1, sl st in blo of each of next 71 (77, 83) sc (ending just before center 15 sts), turn.

Note: Work all scs on RS rows through back (unworked) lp of sc from 2 rows previous.

Row 3: Ch 1, sc in blo of sc from 2 rows previous, sc2tog, sc in each sc to marked st, sc2tog, sc in each sc through marked sc, sc2tog, sc in each sc to last 3 sc, sc2tog, sc in last st, turn—67 (73, 79) sts; 2 Thumb sts dec'd, 2 sts dec'd at Keyhole opening.

Row 4: Ch 1, sl st in blo of each sc across, turn.

Rows 5–10: [Rep Rows 3–4] 3 more times—55 (61, 67) sts.

Row 11: Ch 1, sc in blo of sc from 2 rows previous, sc in each sc to marked st, sc2tog, sc in each sc through marked sc, sc2tog, sc in each sc to end—53 (59, 65) sts.

Row 12: Ch 1, sl st in blo of each sc across, turn.

Rows 13–16: [Rep Rows 11–12] 2 more times—49 (55, 61) sts.

Wristband

Row 1 (RS): Sl st in blo of sc from 2 rows previous, ch 3 (counts as dc), dc in blo of each sc from 2 rows previous across, ch 6 for Wrist Tab, turn.

Row 2 (WS): Ch 1, sl st in blo of second ch from hook and next 4 chs, sl st in blo of each sc across, ch 19 for Wristband, turn.

Note: Work all scs on RS rows through back (unworked) lp of dc or sc from 2 rows previous.

Row 3: Sc through back lp and bottom bump of second ch from hook and next 17 chs, sc in next 49 (55, 61) dc, sc in blo of last 5 sts of free (unworked) ch from 2 rows previous, turn—72 (78, 84) sc.

Row 4: Ch 1, sl st in blo of each sc across, turn.

Row 5: Ch 1, sc in blo of first sc, 2 sc in next sc, sc in each sc to end—73 (79, 84) sc.

Row 6: Ch 1, sl st in blo of each sc across, turn.

Rows 7–8: Rep Rows 5–6—74 (80, 86) sc.

Row 9: Ch 1, sc in blo of first sc, sc in each sc to end, turn.

Row 10: Ch 1, sl st in blo of each sc across, turn.

Row 11: Sl st in blo of sc from 2 rows previous, ch 3 (counts as dc), dc in blo of each sc from 2 rows previous across, turn.

Row 12: Ch 1, sl st in blo of each sc across, turn.

Row 13: Ch 1, sc in blo of first dc from 2 rows previous, sc in each dc to end, turn.

Row 14: Ch 1, sl st in blo of each sc across, turn.

Row 15: Ch 1, sc in blo of first sc, sc2tog, sc in each sc to end, turn—73 (79, 85) sc.

Row 16: Ch 1, sl st in blo of each sc across, turn.

Row 17: Rep Row 15, do not turn—72 (78, 84) sc.

Keyhole Edging

Rotate work 90 degrees clockwise.

Row 1 (RS): Working along side of Wrist Tab, ch 1, work 10 sc evenly along side of Tab, 3 sc in corner, 5 sc along edge of Wrist Tab; working at the rate of 1 sc for every other sc/sl st row, 2 sc for every dc, and 1 sc for every sc, sc evenly around Keyhole opening; working along beg-ch edge of top of Wristband, sc through free lp of beg ch of next 17 sts, work 3 sc in corner, 10 sc evenly along side of Wristband, 2 sc in corner, join with sl st to beg sc from Row 17, turn.

Row 2 (WS): Sl st in blo of each sc along side of Wristband, along top edge, around Keyhole opening, along top edge of Wrist Tab, side of Wrist Tab, and along bottom edge of Row 17 of Cuff, join with sl st to beg sl st, fasten off.

Finishing

Weave in ends. Lightly steam block Wristband and Wrist Tab. Sew one side of snap fastener to RS of Wrist Tab, and the other side to the WS of Wristband. Sew button on the RS of Wristband directly over fastener.

> **TIP:** A standard sized removable stitch marker can be too large for a fine yarn such as Garden Metallic. Try using a very small safety pin or small split ring (typically used in jewelry making). Marking your stitches makes it easy to keep track of where you're at in the pattern!

Spoke
Too
Soon

Round crochet motifs can be so fun looking, but working up dozens of them for an afghan can get old. With this pair of wristers, you're done after just four motifs! When choosing colors for this project, be sure to opt for tones that contrast. The variegated color in this sample, color B, is made up of shades of gray, white, and turquoise. The solid color, A, coordinates and contrasts with it all at once. If using a solid and a variegated color, be sure that the solid does not match any of the shades in the variegated colorway. This will allow the solid color to provide firm spokes around the variegated background.

YARN
Universal Yarn Bamboo Pop, fine weight #2 yarn (50% bamboo, 50% cotton; 292 yds/3.5 oz; 267 m/100 g)
- 1 skein #111 Midnight Blue (A)
- 1 skein #211 Frosty Morning (B)

HOOK AND OTHER MATERIALS
- US E-4 (3.5 mm) crochet hook
- Tapestry needle

GAUGE
22 sts x 22 rows in blo sc = 4"/10 cm square
Be sure to check your gauge!

NOTES
- Change colors using the Fair Isle method; for a photo tutorial, see page 136.
- These mitts are worked in a modular fashion. Both the Back of Hand and Palm are worked separately from the center out using an adjustable ring; for a photo tutorial, see page 122. The Palm is joined to the Back of Hand with slip stitches. The Top Edging and Cuff are worked off the upper and lower circumferences of the hand.

FINISHED MEASUREMENTS
Hand circumference: 7^1/$_2$ (8^1/$_4$, 9)"/19 (21, 23) cm
Length: 5^3/$_4$ (6^1/$_2$, 7^1/$_4$)"/14.5 (16.5, 18.5) cm

SIZES
Women's Small (Medium, Large)
Shown in Small.

Right Mitt

Back of Hand

With A, beg with adjustable ring.

Rnd 1: Ch 3 (counts as dc), 11 dc into ring, with B join with sl st to beg ch-3—12 dc.

Rnd 2: With B, ch 3 (counts as dc), with A, fpdc in 1st dc from Rnd 1, [with B dc in next dc, with A fpdc in same dc] around, with B join with sl st to beg ch 3—12 dc, 12 fpdc.

Rnd 3: With B, ch 3 (counts as dc), dc in same sp, with A fpdc in fpdc from Rnd 2, [with B work 2 dc in next dc, with A fpdc in next fpdc from Rnd 2] around, with B join with sl st to beg ch 3—24 dc, 12 fpdc.

Rnd 4: With B, ch 3 (counts as dc), dc in next dc, work 2 dc in next dc, with A fpdc in fpdc from Rnd 3, [with B dc in next dc, work 2 dc in next dc, with A fpdc in fpdc from Rnd 3] around, with A join with sl st to beg ch 3—36 dc, 12 fpdc.

Rnd 5: With A, turn, sl st in last fpdc made from Rnd 4, turn so RS is facing, ch 5 (counts as dc + ch 2), 2 dc in same sp, {dc in next dc, hdc in next dc, sc in next 7 sts, hdc in next dc, dc in next dc, [2 dc, ch 2, 2 dc] in next fpdc} 3 times, dc in next dc, hdc in next dc, sc in next 7 sts, hdc in next dc, dc in next dc, dc in same st as 1st dc, with B join with sl st to 3rd ch of beg ch 5.

Rnd 6: With B, sl st in ch-2 sp, ch 1, [sc, ch 1, sc] in same sp, {sc in blo of next 15 sts, [sc, ch 1, sc] in next ch-2 sp} 3 times, sc in blo of next 15 sts, with A join with sl st to beg sc.

Rnd 7: With A, sl st in ch-1 sp, ch 1, [sc, ch 1, sc] in same sp, {sc in blo of next 17 sc to ch-1 sp, [sc, ch 1, sc] in next ch-1 sp} 3 times, sc in blo of next 17 sc, with B join with sl st to beg sc.

Rnd 8: With B, sl st in ch-1 sp, ch 1, [sc, ch 1, sc] in same sp, {sc in blo of next 19 sc , [sc, ch 1, sc] in next ch-1 sp} 3 times, sc in blo of next 19 sc, join with sl st to beg sc.

Medium & Large Sizes Only

Rnd 9: With A, sl st in ch-1 sp, ch 1, [sc, ch 1, sc] in same sp, {sc in blo of next 21 sc to ch-1 sp, [sc, ch 1, sc] in next ch-1 sp} 3 times, sc in blo of next 21 sc, with B join with sl st to beg sc.

Rnd 10: With B, sl st in ch-1 sp, ch 1, [sc, ch 1, sc] in same sp, {sc in blo of next 23 sc, [sc, ch 1, sc] in next ch-1 sp} 3 times, sc in blo of next 23 sc, join with sl st to beg sc.

Large Size Only

Rnd 11: With A, sl st in ch-1 sp, ch 1, [sc, ch 1, sc] in same sp, {sc in blo of next 25 sc to ch-1 sp, [sc, ch 1, sc] in next ch-1 sp} 3 times, sc in blo of next 25 sc, with B join with sl st to beg sc.

Rnd 12: With B, sl st in ch-1 sp, ch 1, [sc, ch 1, sc] in same sp, {sc in blo of next 27 sc, [sc, ch 1, sc] in next ch-1 sp} 3 times, sc in blo of next 27 sc, join with sl st to beg sc.

All Sizes

Fasten off.

Palm

With A, begin with adjustable ring.

Rnd 1: Ch 3 (counts as dc), 11 dc into ring, with B join with sl st to beg ch-3—12 dc.

Rnd 2: Ch 3 (counts as dc), dc in same sp, [2 dc in next dc] around, join with sl st to beg ch-3—24 dc.

Rnd 3: Ch 3 (counts as dc), 2 dc in next dc, [dc in next dc, 2 dc in next dc] around, join with sl st to beg ch-3—36 dc.

Rnd 4: Ch 3 (counts as dc), dc in next dc, 2 dc in next dc, [dc in next 2 dc, 2 dc in next dc] around, join with sl st to beg ch-3—48 dc.

Rnd 5: Ch 5 (counts as dc + ch 2), 2 dc in same sp, {dc in next dc, hdc in next dc, sc in next 7 dc, hdc in next dc, dc in next dc, [2 dc, ch 2, 2 dc] in next dc} 3 times, dc in next dc, hdc in next dc, sc in next 7 dc, hdc in next dc, dc in next dc, dc in same st as 1st dc, with B join with sl st to 3rd ch of beg ch 5.

Rnd 6: Sl st in next ch-2 sp, ch 4 (counts as dc + ch 1), 2 dc in same sp, dc in next 15 sts, {[2 dc, ch 1, 2 dc] in next ch-2 sp, dc in next 15 sts} 3 times, dc in same sp as beg ch-5, join with sl st to 3rd ch of beg ch-5.

Rnd 7: Sl st in ch-2 sp, ch 1, [sc, ch 1, sc] in same sp, {sc in blo of next 19 dc, [sc, ch 1, sc] in next ch-1 sp} 3 times, sc in blo of next 19 dc, join with sl st to beg sc.

Medium & Large Sizes Only

Rnd 8: Sl st in ch-2 sp, ch 1, [sc, ch 1, sc] in same sp, {sc in blo of next 21 dc, [sc, ch 1, sc] in next ch-1 sp} 3 times, sc in blo of next 21 dc, join with sl st to beg sc.

Rnd 9: Sl st in ch-2 sp, ch 1, [sc, ch 1, sc] in same sp, {sc in blo of next 23 dc, [sc, ch 1, sc] in next ch-1 sp} 3 times, sc in blo of next 23 dc, join with sl st to beg sc.

Large Size Only

Rnd 10: Sl st in ch-2 sp, ch 1, [sc, ch 1, sc] in same sp, {sc in blo of next 25 dc, [sc, ch 1, sc] in next ch-1 sp} 3 times, sc in blo of next 25 dc, join with sl st to beg sc.

Rnd 11: Sl st in ch-2 sp, ch 1, [sc, ch 1, sc] in same sp, {sc in blo of next 27 dc, [sc, ch 1, sc] in next ch-1 sp} 3 times, sc in blo of next 27 dc, join with sl st to beg sc.

All Sizes

Do not fasten off.

Join Back of Hand and Palm, Right Hand Side

With yarn still attached to Palm, hold Back of Hand and Palm with WS tog, with Back of Hand facing you.

Row 1: Working through blo of each sc on Back of Hand and flo of each Palm sc, sl st corner chs tog, sl st next 21 sc tog, sl st next corner chs tog. Fasten off.

Join Back of Hand and Palm, Left Hand (Thumb) Side

Hold Back of Hand and Palm with WS tog, with RS of Back of Hand facing you. Rotate work so you are joining the edge parallel to the edge just joined.

Row 1: Working through blo of each sc on both pieces, sl st corner chs tog, sl st next 4 (5, 6) sc tog, working along Palm piece only, sl st loosely in next 13 (15, 17) sc; sk 13 (15, 17) sc from Back of Hand piece; working through both pieces again, sl st next 4 (5, 6) sc tog, sl st corner chs tog. Do not fasten off.

Top Edging

Rnd 1: Ch 1, sc in blo of same ch, sc in blo of next 21 (25, 29) sc along Palm piece, sc in blo of corner ch; working along Back of Hand, sc in blo of corner ch, sc in blo of next 21 (25, 29) sc, sc in blo of corner ch, join with sl st to beg sc—46 (54, 62) sc.

Rnds 2–3: Ch 1, sc in blo of same sc, sc in blo of each sc around, join with sl st to beg sc. Fasten off.

Cuff

With RS Hand facing, attach A to corner ch of either edge.

Rnd 1: Ch 1, sc in blo of same ch, sc in blo of next 21 (25, 29) sc along Palm piece, sc in blo of corner ch; working along Back of Hand, sc in blo of corner ch, sc in blo of next 21 (25, 29) sc, sc in blo of corner ch, join with sl st to beg sc—46 (54, 62) sc.

Small Size Only

Rnd 2: Ch 1, sc in same sp, sc in next sc, [sc2tog, sc in next 6 sc] 4 times, sc2tog, sc in next 4 sc, sc2tog, sc in last 2 sc, with B join with sl st to beg sc—40 sc.

Medium Size Only

Rnd 2: Ch 1, sc in same sp, sc in next sc, [sc2tog, sc in next 5 sc] 6 times, sc2tog, sc in next 4 sc, sc2tog, sc in last sc, with B join with sl st to beg sc—46 sc.

Large Size Only:

Rnd 2: Ch 1, sc in same sp, sc in next 2 sc [sc2tog, sc in next 4 sc] 9 times, sc2tog, sc in last 3 sc, with B join with sl st to top of beg ch-3—52 sc.

All Sizes

Rnd 3: With B, ch 1, sc in each sc around, with A join with sl st to beg sc.

Rnd 4: Ch 1, fpdc around sc from 2 rnds below, ch 1, [fpdc around next sc from 2 rnds below] around, with B join with sl st to beg dc.

Rnd 5: Ch 1, dc in 1st sc from Rnd 3, [dc in next sc from Rnd 3] around, with A join with sl st to beg dc.

Rnd 6: Ch 1, fpdc in fpdc from 2 rnds below, ch 3, sl st in 2nd and then 3rd chs from hook, [fpdc in next fpdc from 2 rnds below, ch 3, sl st in 2nd and then 3rd chs from hook] around, with B join with sl st to beg dc.

Rnd 7: Ch 1, dc in dc from 2 rnds below, dc in next 19 (22, 25) dc around, sl st in back bar of corresponding fpdc from last rnd, dc in last 20 (23, 26) dc from 2 rnds below, join with sl st to beg dc. Fasten off.

Thumb Edging

Attach A to lower Thumb opening. Sl st evenly in blo of each sc around, fasten off.

Left Mitt

Back of Hand and Palm

Work as for Right Mitt.

Join Back of Hand and Palm, Left Hand Side

With yarn still attached to Palm, hold Back of Hand and Palm with WS tog, with Back of Hand facing you.

Row 1: Working through blo of each sc on Back of Hand and flo of each Palm sc, sl st corner chs tog, sl st next 21 sc tog, sl st next corner chs tog, do not fasten off.

Join Back of Hand and Palm, Right Hand (Thumb) Side

Hold Back of Hand and Palm with WS tog, with RS of Back of Hand facing you. Rotate work so you are joining the edge parallel to the edge just joined.

Row 1: Working through blo of each sc on both pieces, sl st corner chs tog, sl st next 4 (5, 6) sc tog, working along Palm piece only, sl st loosely in next 13 (15, 17) sc; sk 13 (15, 17) sc from Back of Hand piece; working through both pieces again, sl st next 4 (5, 6) sc tog, sl st corner chs tog. Fasten off.

Top Edging, Cuff, Thumb

Work as for Right Mitt.

Finishing

Weave in ends. Steam block to relax edging.

Ode to Bruges

Bruges lace gets its name from a bobbin lace that was made in Bruges in the seventeenth and eighteenth centuries. Characteristically it has scrolling curves separated by a mesh texture. This mitt pattern is an adaptation of much crochet Bruges lace seen in the pattern world, but with a twist. In most crochet Bruges lace patterns, double crochet rows end with chain spaces that attach to the previous rows' chain spaces. In this version, subtle shaping in the double crochet rows makes for a narrow wrist and slightly flared cuff, allowing this project to "fit like a glove."

FINISHED MEASUREMENTS
Hand circumference: 6³/₄"/17 cm
Length: 5³/₄"/14.5 cm

SIZE
Women's Small

YARN
Fibra Natura Whisper Lace, super fine #1 yarn (70% wool, 30% silk; 440 yds/1.75 oz; 402 m/50 g)
• 1 ball #113 Tango

HOOK AND OTHER MATERIALS
• US steel 7 (1.65 mm) crochet hook
• Tapestry needle

GAUGE
28 sts x 14 rows in dc = 4"/10 cm square
Be sure to check your gauge!

NOTES

- To help keep track of the right and wrong sides of the work, try attaching a safety pin or split ring marker to the right side after the first few rows.

Right Mitt

Ch 7.

Row 1 (RS): Dc in 6th ch from hook, dc in last ch, ch 5, turn.

Rows 2–5: Dc in each dc, ch 5, turn—2 dc.

Row 6 (WS): Work 2 dc in 1st dc, dc in next dc, ch 5, turn—3 dc.

Rows 7–13: Dc in each dc, ch 5, turn.

Row 14: Work 2 dc in 1st dc, dc in next 2 dc, ch 5, turn—4 dc.

Row 15: Dc in each dc, ch 5, turn.

Row 16: Dc in 1st 2 dc, hdc in next dc, sc in last dc, turn.

Row 17: Ch 1, sc in sc, hdc in hdc, dc in last 2 dc, ch 5, turn.

Row 18: Dc in 1st 2 dc, hdc in hdc, sc in sc, turn.

Rows 19–20: Rep Rows 17–18.

Row 21: Rep Row 17.

Row 22: Dc in 1st 2 dc, hdc in hdc, sc in sc, ch 2, sl st in third 3rd ch of corresponding ch-5 sp, ch 2, turn.

Row 23: Dc in each st, ch 5, turn.

Row 24: Dc2tog, dc in last 2 dc, ch 2, sl st in 3rd ch of corresponding ch-5 sp, ch 2, turn—3 dc.

Rows 25–30: [Rep Rows 23–24] 3 times.

Row 31: Rep Row 23.

Row 32: Dc2tog, dc in last dc, ch 2, sl st in 3rd ch of corresponding ch-5 sp, ch 2, turn—2 dc.

Row 33: Dc in each dc, ch 5, turn.

Row 34: Dc in each dc, ch 2, sl st in 3rd ch of corresponding ch-5 sp, ch 2, turn.

Rows 35–36: Rep Rows 33–34.

Row 37: Rep Row 33.

Row 38: Work 2 dc in 1st dc, dc in next dc, ch 5, turn—3 dc.

Rows 39–40: Dc in each dc, ch 5, turn.

Row 41: Dc in 1st dc, hdc in next dc, sc in last dc, turn.

Row 42: Ch 1, sc in sc, hdc in hdc, dc in dc, ch 5, turn.

Rows 43–44: Rep Rows 41–42.

Row 45: Dc in dc, hdc in hdc, sc in sc, ch 2, sl st in 3rd ch of corresponding ch-5 sp, ch 2, turn.

Row 46: Dc in each dc, ch 5, turn.

Row 47: Dc in each dc, ch 2, sl st in 3rd ch of corresponding ch-5 sp, ch 2, turn.

Row 48: Dc2tog, dc in last dc, ch 5—2 dc.

Row 49: Dc in each dc, ch 2, sl st in 3rd ch of corresponding ch-5 sp, ch 2, turn.

Row 50: Dc in each dc, ch 5, turn.

Rows 51–52: Rep Rows 49–50.

Row 53: Rep Row 49.

Row 54: Work 2 dc in 1st dc, dc in next dc, ch 5, turn—3 dc.

Row 55: Dc in each dc, ch 2, sl st in 3rd ch of corresponding ch-5 sp, ch 2, turn.

Row 56: Dc in each dc, ch 5, turn.

Rows 57–60: [Rep Rows 55–56] 2 times.

Row 61: Rep Row 55.

Row 62: Work 2 dc in 1st dc, dc in next 2 dc, ch 5, turn—4 dc.

Rows 63–95: Rep Rows 15–47.

Row 96: Dc2tog, dc in last dc, ch 2, turn—2 dc.

Row 97: Dc in each dc, ch 2, sl st in 3rd ch of corresponding ch-5 sp, ch 2, turn.

Row 98: Dc in each dc, ch 2, turn.

Rows 99–100: Rep Rows 97–98.

Row 101: Rep Row 97.

Row 102: Work 2 dc in 1st dc, dc in next dc, ch 2, turn—3 dc.

Rows 103–104: Rep Rows 97–98.

Row 105: Rep Row 97.

Rows 106–123: Rep Rows 58–75.

Row 124: Dc in each dc, ch 2, turn.

Row 125: Dc in each dc, ch 5, turn.

Rows 126–127: Rep Rows 124–125.

Row 128: Dc2tog, dc in last dc, ch 2, turn—2 dc.

Row 129: Dc in each dc, ch 5, turn.

Row 130: Dc in each dc, ch 2, turn.

Rows 131–132: Rep Rows 129–130.

Row 133: Rep Row 129.

Row 134: 2 dc in 1st dc, dc in next dc, ch 2, sl st in 3rd ch of corresponding ch-5 sp, ch 2, turn.

Rows 135–182: Rep Rows 39–86.

Rows 183–212: Rep Rows 39–68.

Row 213: Ch 1, sc in sc, hdc in hdc, dc in last 2 dc, ch 2, sl st in 3rd ch of ch-5 sp from Row 16 (from first column, thereby joining mitt), ch 2, turn.

Rows 214–240: Cont in patt as est'd, joining end of RS rows to first column. Fasten off, leaving 4"/10 cm tail. Sew tops of last dcs worked to bottom of dcs from Row 1.

Left Mitt

Work as for Right Mitt.

Finishing

Top Edging

Join yarn to sp indicated by arrow in chart.

Rnd 1: Ch 1, sc in same st, 2 sc in next ch-2 sp, 2 sc in side of next dc, 5 sc in next ch-5 sp, 2 sc in side of next dc, 5 sc in next ch-5 sp, 2 sc in side of next dc, 2 sc in next ch-2 sp, [sc in next sl st, 2 sc in next ch-2 sp, 2 sc in side of next dc, 5 sc in next ch-5 sp, 2 sc in side of next dc, 5 sc in next ch-5 sp, 2 sc in side of next dc, 2 sc in next ch-2 sp] 4 times, join with sl st to beg sc. Fasten off.

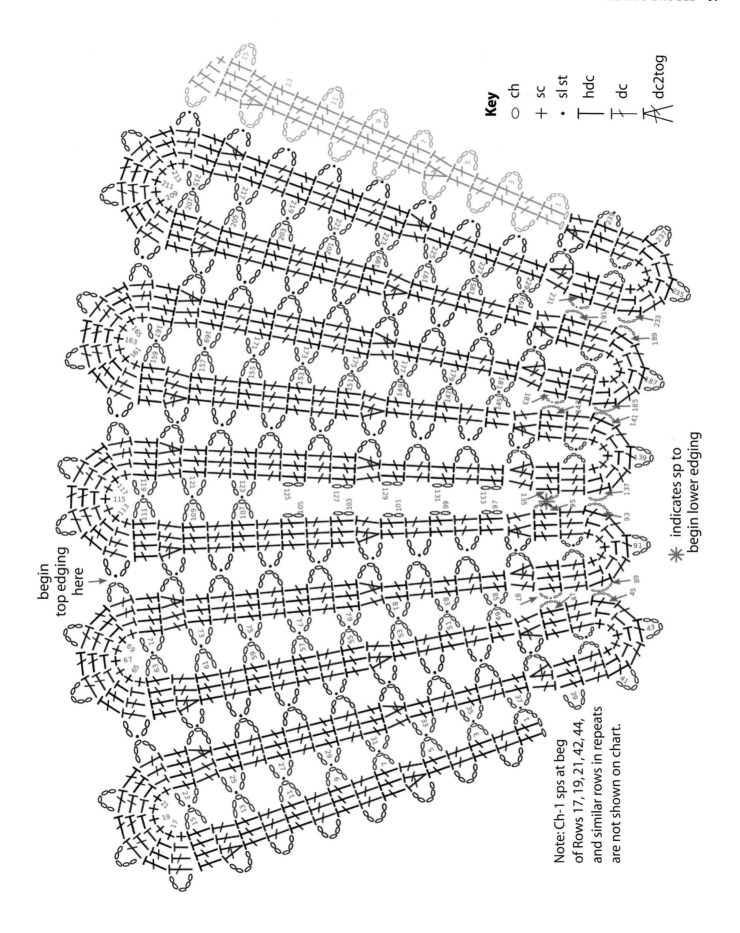

Key
○ ch
+ sc
• sl st
T hdc
F dc
⅀ dc2tog

begin
top edging
here →

✳ indicates sp to
begin lower edging

Note: Ch-1 sps at beg
of Rows 17, 19, 21, 42, 44,
and similar rows in repeats
are not shown on chart.

Thumb Edging

Join yarn to lower opening of thumb opening.

Rnd 1: Ch 1, work 2 sc along side of each row around entire opening, join with sl st to beg sc—44 sc.

Rnd 2: Sc in same sc and each sc around, join with sl st to beg sc. Fasten off.

Lower Edging

Join yarn to sp indicated by asterisk in chart.

Rnd 1: Ch 1, sc in same st, 2 sc in ch-2 sp, [2 sc in side of next dc, 5 sc in next ch-5 sp] 3 times, 2 sc in ch-2 sp, {sc in next sl st, 2 sc in ch-2 sp, [2 sc in side of next dc, 5 sc in next ch-5 sp] 3 times, 2 sc in ch-2 sp} 4 times, join with sl st to beg sc. Fasten off.

Weave in ends. Wet block to open up lace and even out edging.

> **TIP:** As written, this pattern fits a small-sized hand using lace weight yarn. Try using a heavier weight of yarn such as sock weight to fit a slightly larger hand.

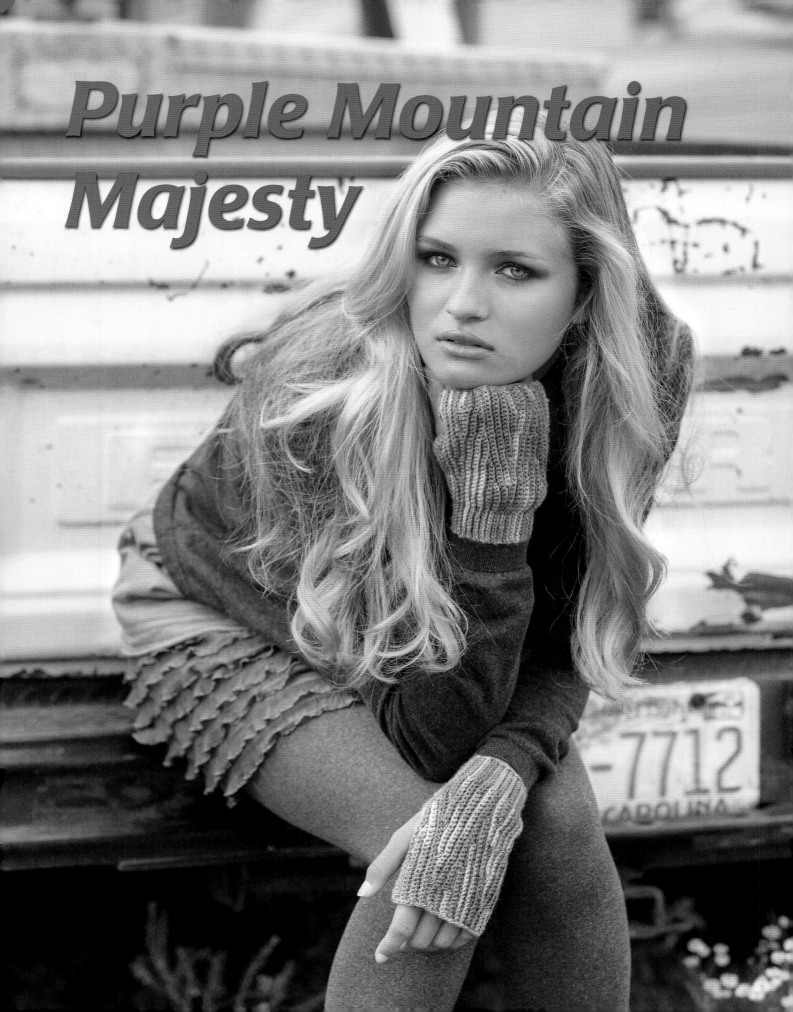

Purple Mountain Majesty

These stretchy mitts are inspired by the Tennessee Smoky Mountains. Worked in back loop single crochet, short rows take you back and forth across your work, just like hiking switchbacks on a treacherous rocky trail.

FINISHED MEASUREMENTS
Hand circumference: 7 (8³/₄)"/18 (22) cm
Length: 6 (6³/₄)"/15 (17) cm

SIZES
Women's Small (Medium/Large)
Shown in Small.

YARN
Deborah Norville Collection Serenity Sock by Premier Yarns, super fine #1 yarn (50% superwash merino wool, 25% bamboo, 25% nylon; 230 yds/1.75 oz; 210 m/50 g)
• 1 skein #DN108-01 Lavender Topaz

HOOK AND OTHER MATERIALS
• US D-3 (3.25 mm) crochet hook
• Tapestry needle

GAUGE
27 sts x 34 rows in blo sc = 4"/10 cm square
Be sure to check your gauge!

NOTES
• This mitt is worked sideways in one piece and is shaped using short rows. See page 142 for a photo tutorial.

STITCH PATTERN
Slip Stitch Ribbing (any number of sts)
Row 1 (RS): Sc in second ch from hook and each ch across.
Row 2 (WS): Loosely sl st in blo of each sc across.
Row 3: Working behind sl sts from previous row, sc in blo (the unworked loop) of each sc from 2 rows below across.
Rep Rows 2–3 for patt.

Right Mitt

Ch 41 (46).

Short-Row Section 1

Row 1 (RS): Working through blo of each ch, work Row 1 of Slip Stitch Ribbing over 10 sts, sc in next 24 (28) chs—34 (38) sc, 6 (7) chs left unworked.

WS Rows 2–8: Ch 1, sc in blo of each sc to last 10 sts, work Row 2 of Slip Stitch Ribbing over 10 sts, turn.

Row 3: Ch 1, work Row 3 of Slip Stitch Ribbing over 10 sts, sc in blo of next 18 (21) sc, turn.

Row 5: Ch 1, work Row 3 of Slip Stitch Ribbing over 10 sts, sc in blo of next 12 (14) sc, turn.

Row 7: Ch 1, work Row 3 of Slip Stitch Ribbing over 10 sts, sc in blo of next 6 (7) sc, turn.

Row 9: Ch 1, work Row 3 of Slip Stitch Ribbing over 10 sts, sc in blo of next 6 (7) sc, [work next sc tog with t-ch-1 in blo of sc, sc in blo of next 5 (6) sc] 3 times, work next ch tog with t-ch-1 in blo of sc, sc in blo of last 5 (6) chs, turn.

Row 10: Ch 1, sc in blo of next 30 (35) sc, work Row 2 of Slip Stitch Ribbing over last 10 sts, turn.

Row 11: Ch 1, work Row 3 of Slip Stitch Ribbing over 10 sts, sc in blo of each sc to end, turn.

Row 12: Ch 1, sc in blo of next 24 (28) sc, turn.

RS Rows 13–19: Ch 1, sc in blo of each sc to end, turn.

Row 14: Ch 1, sc in blo of next 18 (21) sc, turn.

Row 16: Ch 1, sc in blo of next 12 (14) sc, turn.

Row 18: Ch 1, sc in blo of next 6 (7) sc, turn.

Row 20: Ch 1, sc in blo of next 6 (7) sc, [work next sc tog with t-ch-1 in blo of sc, sc in blo of next 5 (6) sc] 4 times, work Row 2 of Slip Stitch Ribbing over last 10 sts, turn.

Row 21: Ch 1, work Row 3 of Slip Stitch Ribbing over 10 sts, sc in blo of each sc to end, turn.

Row 22: Ch 1, sc in blo of next 30 (35) sc, work Row 2 of Slip Stitch Ribbing over last 10 sts, turn.

Short-Row Section 2

Row 1 (RS): Work Row 1 of Slip Stitch Ribbing over 10 sts, sc in blo of next 24 (28) sc—34 (38) sc, 6 (7) chs left unworked.

Rows 2–22: Work as for Short-Row Section 1.

Short-Row Section 3

[Rep Short-Row Section 2] 1 (2) times.

Short-Row Section 4

Rep Rows 1–21 of Short-Row Section 2.

Join Mitt

With WS of working row facing, bring beg-ch edge up and parallel with work so both WS are tog.

Note: When joining mitt, work through blo of last row worked and through both free loops of beg-ch edge.

Next row: Ch 1, insert hook through 1st ch of beg-ch edge, insert hook through 1st sc on last row worked, sc

through both layers, insert hook through next ch from beg-ch edge and next sc from last row worked, sc through both layers, work 9 (11) more sc in this way—11 (13) sc formed so far; working through beg-ch edge only, sc in each of next 14 (17) chs, sk next 14 (17) sc of working row (this forms a hole for the thumb to fit through), working through both layers again, work 5 sc; working through both layers, sl st in last 10 sts. Fasten off.

Left Mitt

Work as for Right Mitt.

Finishing

Join yarn to bottom of thumb opening, sl st loosely in blo of each st around opening. Fasten off.

Upper Edging

Attach yarn to upper edge. Sl st loosely in the side of each row around. Fasten off.

Weave in ends.

Emotimitts

Wear your heart on your sleeve, er, hand with these emotion-bearing mitts. Are you having a mixed-emotions kind of day? No problem. Just wear a different emoticon on each hand. With their velcro adhesion, you can let the world know precisely how you're feeling at any given moment. A few ideas are provided to get you started on the emotive embroidery. Take it from there and stitch your own personal feelings onto these little circles!

FINISHED MEASUREMENTS
Hand circumference: 7^1/$_4$ (8^1/$_4$, 9^1/$_4$)"/18.5 (21, 23.5) cm
Length: 6 (6^1/$_2$, 7)"/15 (16.5, 18) cm

SIZES
Women's Small (Medium, Large)
Shown in Small.

YARN
Deborah Norville Collection Everyday Soft Worsted by Premier Yarns, medium weight #4 yarn (100% anti-pilling acrylic; 203 yds/4 oz; 186 m/113 g)

- 1 skein #ED100-32 Peony (MC)
- 1 skein #ED100-27 Lemon (CC1)
- 1 skein #ED100-12 Black (CC2)

HOOKS AND OTHER MATERIALS
- US 7 (4.5 mm) crochet hook
- US G-6 (4 mm) crochet hook
- Tapestry needle
- Sewing needle and black thread
- Sew-on Velcro

GAUGE
14 sts x 14 rows in Doubles patt = 4"/10 cm square using larger hook
Be sure to check your gauge!

NOTES
- See page 122 for a photo tutorial on making an adjustable ring.
- See page 137 for a photo tutorial on making faux French knots, used as eyes on the Emoticons.

STITCH PATTERNS
Doubles (worked in joined rows)
(odd number of sts)
Row 1: Ch 1, sc in same sc, [sk next sc, 2 sc in next sc] across, join with sl st to beg sc, turn.
Rep for patt.

Doubles (worked in unjoined rows)
(odd number of sts)
Row 1: Ch 1, sc in same sc, [sk next sc, 2 sc in next sc] across, turn.
Rep for patt.

Right Mitt

With MC and larger hook, ch 25 (29, 33), join with sl st in bottom bump of 1st ch to form ring.
Row 1: Ch 1, sc in bottom bump of each ch across, join with sl st to beg sc, turn.
Work Row 1 of Doubles patt in joined rows 3 times.

Thumb Opening

Work Row 1 of Doubles patt in unjoined rows 9 (10, 11) times.

Upper Hand

Work Row 1 of Doubles patt in joined rows 8 (9, 10) times. Fasten off.

Thumb

Attach yarn at upper edge of opening.
Row 1 (RS): Ch 1, work 18 (20, 22) sc evenly around opening, turn.
Row 2 (WS): Ch 1, sl st in each of next 3 (4, 4) sc, sc in each of next 2 (2, 3) sc, hdc in each of next 2 sc, dc in next 4 sc, hdc in next 2 sc, sc in next 2 (2, 3) sc, sl st in last 3 (4, 4) sc, join with sl st to beg sl st, turn.
Row 3: Ch 1, sl st in next 3 (4, 4) sl st, sc in next 2 (2, 3) sc, hdc2tog, dc in next 4 dc, hdc2tog, sc in next 2 (2, 3) sc, sl st in last 3 (4, 4) sl st, join with sl st to beg sl st, turn—16 (18, 20) sts.
Row 4: Loosely sl st in each st around. Fasten off.

Left Mitt

Work as for Right Mitt.

Emoticons

Base Circle

With CC1 and smaller hook, begin with adjustable ring.
Rnd 1: Ch 1, work 6 sc in ring, join with sl st to beg sc.
Rnd 2: Ch 1, work 2 sc in same sc and in each sc around, join with sl st to beg sc—12 sc.
Rnd 3: Ch 1, sc in same sc, 2 sc in next sc, [sc in next sc, 2 sc in next sc] around, join with sl st to beg sc—18 sc.
Rnd 4: Ch 1, 2 sc in same sc and in next 2 sc, [2 sc in next sc, sc in next 2 sc] around, join with sl st to beg sc—24 sc. Fasten off.
Turn Base Circle over so WS is facing. This will be the right side of the work.

Emoticons

Grin   Unsure

Surprised   Winking

Key

faux French knot

tack down with sewing thread

CC2

Base Circle Edging

Rnd 1: With CC2 and smaller hook, beginning with any sc from Rnd 4 of Base Circle, sl st in blo of each sc around. Fasten off.

Embroidery

For embroidery on each pair of Emoticons, cut a 12"/30.5 cm length of CC2. Embroider Emoticons using diagrams and photos as a guide. For eyes on each Emoticon, use faux French knots (see page 137). Black lines on Emoticons indicate CC2. Use black sewing thread to tack down CC2 in locations indicated on diagram.

Finishing

Weave in ends.
For each Emoticon, cut two pieces of the fuzzy portion of the Velcro 3/8"/1 cm long. Sew pieces to back of Emoticon at top and bottom, invisibly, using a whipstitch. Position Emoticon on the back of each mitt to determine placement for the other Velcro pieces. For each mitt, cut two pieces of the prickly portion of the Velcro, also 3/8"/1 cm long. Sew pieces to back of mitt.

Horizon

This fingerless mitt project is the perfect way to use a special skein of sock yarn. Shown in a striping yarn, these mitts will look great in a solid colorway as well. Front post stitches create the ridged look in an easy-to-follow four-row pattern repeat.

FINISHED MEASUREMENTS
Hand circumference: $7^{1}/_{4}$ ($8^{1}/_{4}$, $9^{1}/_{4}$)"/18 (21, 23.5) cm
Length: $6^{3}/_{4}$ (8, 9)"/17 (20.5, 23) cm

SIZES
Women's Small (Medium, Large)
Shown in Small.

YARN
Wisdom Yarns Saki Silk, super fine #1 yarn (50% superwash merino wool, 25% silk, 25% nylon; 440 yds/3.5 oz; 210 m/50 g)
• 1 skein #303 Peach Cobbler

HOOK AND OTHER MATERIALS
• US B-1 (2.25 mm) crochet hook
• Tapestry needle

GAUGE

30 sts x 32 rows in blo sc = 4"/10 cm square

3 reps of Ridged Circles patt = 2³/4"/7 cm wide x 3¹/2"/9 cm high

Be sure to check your gauge!

NOTES

- First the cuff is worked side to side and seamed.
- The hand is worked in joined rows around the side edge of the cuff.

STITCH GUIDE

7-fpdc sh

Yo, insert hook around post of next st from front to back, yo and pull up a lp (3 lps on hook), yo and pull through 2 lps (2 lps on hook), [yo, insert hook around post of next st from front to back, yo and pull up a lp, yo and pull through 2 lps] 6 times (8 lps on hook), yo and pull through all lps on hook, ch 1 to close.

4-fpdc sh

Yo, insert hook around post of next st from front to back, yo and pull up a lp (3 lps on hook), yo and pull through 2 lps (2 lps on hook), [yo, insert hook around post of next st from front to back, yo and pull up a lp, yo and pull through 2 lps] 3 times (5 lps on hook), yo and pull through all lps on hook, ch 1 to close.

3-fpdc sh

Yo, insert hook around post of next st from front to back, yo and pull up a lp (3 lps on hook), yo and pull through 2 lps (2 lps on hook), [yo, insert hook around post of next st from front to back, yo and pull up a lp, yo and pull through 2 lps] 2 times (4 lps on hook), yo, and pull through all lps on hook, ch 1 to close.

STITCH PATTERNS

Ridged Circles (worked in joined rows)

(multiple of 8 sts)

Set-up row (RS): Ch 3 (counts as dc), work 3 dc in same st, sk next 2 sts, [sc in next st, sk next 2 sc, 7 dc in next st, sk next 2 sc] 7 (8, 9) times, sc in next st, sk last 2 sts, 3 dc in same st as beg dc, join with sl st to top of beg dc, turn— 8 (9, 10) 7-dc groups, 8 (9, 10) sc.

Row 1 (WS): Ch 3 (does not count as dc), [7-fpdc sh, ch 3, fpsc in next dc, ch 3] 7 (8, 9) times, 7-fpdc sh, ch 3, fpsc in last dc, join with sl st to beg ch, turn.

Row 2: Ch 1, sc in same sc, [7 dc in top of next sh, sc in next sc] 7 (8, 9) times, 7 dc in top of next sh, join with sl st to beg sc, turn.

Row 3: Ch 1, fpslst around same sc, ch 3 (counts as center of fpdc sh), 3-fpdc sh, ch 3, fpsc in next dc, ch 3 [7-fpdc sh, ch 3, fpsc in next dc, ch 3] 7 (8, 9) times, 3-fpdc sh, join with sl st to top of beg sh, turn.

Ridged Circles
(worked back and forth in rows)

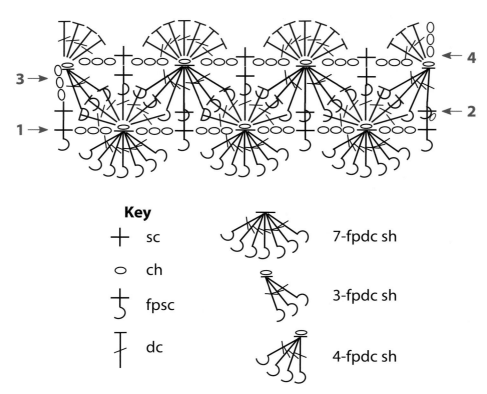

Key

+ sc

o ch

� fpsc

⊤ dc

7-fpdc sh

3-fpdc sh

4-fpdc sh

Row 4: Ch 3 (counts as dc), 3 dc in same sh, [sc in next sc, 7 dc in top of next sh] 7 (8, 9) times, sc in next sc, 3 dc in same sh as beg 3 dc, join with sl st to top of beg dc, turn.
Rep Rows 1–4 for patt.

Ridged Circles (worked back and forth in rows)
(multiple of 8 sts + 1)
(follow these instructions when working back and forth for the thumb opening)
Row 1 (WS): Ch 1, fpsc in same st, ch 3 (does not count as dc), [7-fpdc sh, ch 3, fpsc in next dc, ch 3] 7 (8, 9) times, 7-fpdc sh, ch 3, fpsc in last dc, turn—8 (9, 10) sh, 10 (12, 14) fpsc.
Row 2 (RS): Ch 1, sc in same sc, [7 dc in top of next sh, sc in next sc] 7 (8, 9) times, 7 dc in top of next sh, sc in last sc, turn.
Row 3: Ch 1, fpslst around same sc, ch 3 (counts as first st of sh), 3-fpdc sh, ch 3, fpsc in next dc, ch 3, [7-fpdc sh, ch 3, fpsc in next dc, ch 3] 7 (8, 9) times, 4-fpdc sh, turn.
Row 4: Ch 3 (counts as dc), 3 dc in same st, [sc in next sc, 7 dc in top of next sh] 7 (8, 9) times, sc in next sc, 4 dc in last sh, turn.
Rep Rows 1–4 for patt.

Right Mitt

Cuff
Ch 15.
Row 1: Sc in blo of 2nd ch from hook and each ch across, turn—14 (16, 18) sc.
Row 2: Ch 1, sc in blo of same sc, sc in blo of each sc across, turn.
Rows 3–48: [Rep Row 2] 46 (54, 62) times.
Joining row: Ch 1, working through blo of last Cuff row worked and both free loops of beg ch1, sl st ends of cuff tog. Fasten off. Turn Cuff right side out.

Hand
With Cuff seam centered and face up, count 10 rows to the right, join yarn at the edge.
Rnd 1: Ch 1, treating the ends of the rows as sts, sc in same row, sc in each row around, join with sl st to beg sc—48 (56, 64) sc.
Work Set-up row of Ridged Circles patt (worked in joined rows). Work Rows 1–3 of Ridged Circles patt (worked in joined rows).

Thumb Opening
Work Row 4 of Ridged Circles patt (worked back and forth in rows)—49 (57, 65) sts.

Small Size Only
Work Rows 1–4 of Ridged Circles patt (worked back and forth in rows).

Rep Rows 1–3.
Next row: Work Row 4 of Ridged Circles patt (worked in joined rows)—48 sts.
Cont to work in patt in joined rows for 6 more rows, ending with Row 2. Do not turn.

Medium Size Only
Work Rows 1–4 of Ridged Circles patt (worked back and forth in rows) 2 times
Rep Row 1.
Next row: Work Row 2 of Ridged Circles patt (worked in joined rows)—56 sts.
Cont to work in patt in joined rows for 8 more rows, ending with Row 2. Do not turn.

Large Size Only
Work Rows 1–4 of Ridged Circles patt (worked back and forth in rows) 2 times.
Rep Rows 1–3.
Next row: Work Row 4 of Ridged Circles patt (worked in joined rows)—64 sts.
Cont to work in patt in joined rows for 10 more rows in patt, ending with Row 2. Do not turn.

All Sizes
Next rnd: Ch 1, sl st in blo of each st around, join with sl st to beg sl st. Fasten off.

Left Mitt

Cuff
Work as for Right Mitt.

Hand
With Cuff seam centered and face up, count 10 rows to the left, join yarn at the edge.

Thumb Opening
Complete as for Right Mitt.

Finishing

Weave in ends.

Catch the Wave

A variegated yarn plays the starring role in this pair of fingerless mitts. Colorful yarns can look great on the ball or skein but don't always look as wonderful worked up into a project. This pattern is designed to make the most of a short-repeat variegated yarn, using a simple linen stitch to show it off. Top it off with slip stitch-appliquéd waves, and you've got yourself a beach party!

FINISHED MEASUREMENTS

Hand circumference: 6 (7¼)"/15 (18.5) cm [stretches to 7 (8.5)"/18 (21.5) cm]
Length: 8 (9)"/20.5 (23) cm

SIZES

Women's Small (Medium/Large)
Shown in Small.

YARN

Premier Yarns Ever Soft, medium weight #4 yarn (100% acrylic; 158 yds/3 oz; 144.5 m/85 g)
• 1 ball #70-23 Clover (A)
Premier Yarns Ever Soft Multi, medium weight #4 yarn (100% acrylic; 130 yds/2.47 oz; 119 m/70 g)
• 1 ball #36-06 Surfboard (B)

HOOKS AND OTHER MATERIALS

• US E-4 (3.5 mm) crochet hook
• US G-6 (4 mm) crochet hook
• Tapestry needle
• Sewing needle and thread

GAUGE

Using smaller hook, 24 sts x 32 rows in Slip Stitch Ribbing = 4"/10 cm square
Using larger hook, 20 sts x 16 rows in Linen Stitch patt = 4"/10 cm square
Be sure to check your gauge!

NOTES

• The cuff is worked sideways and is left unjoined.
• The hand is worked off the side of the cuff.
• When working Linen Stitch patt in the hand section, let the unused color hang from the work. Carry the colors up each round.

STITCH PATTERNS

Slip Stitch Ribbing (worked over any number of sts)
Row 1 (RS): Sc in 2nd ch from hook and each ch across.
Row 2 (WS): Loosely sl st in blo of each sc across.
Row 3: Working behind sl sts from previous row, sc in blo (the unworked lp) of each sc from 2 rows below across.
Rep Rows 2–3 for patt.

Linen Stitch (even number of sts)
Patt row: [Sc in next ch-1 sp, ch 1, sk next sc] across.

Right Mitt

Cuff

With A and smaller hook, ch 14.
Work Rows 1–3 of Slip Stitch Ribbing.
[Rep Rows 2–3] 20 (24) more times.

Rep Row 2—22 (26) "ridges."
Next row (RS): Ch 1, sl st in blo of same sl st, ch 28, working through bottom bump of each ch, sl st in 2nd ch from hook and next 26 chs (Lower Right Wave made), sl st in blo of next 7 sl sts, ch 28, working through bottom bump of each ch, sl st in 2nd ch from hook and next 26 chs (Upper Right Wave made), sl st in last 5 chs, ch 1, turn work 90 degrees clockwise, work 45 (54) sl sts along side of Cuff (about 1 sl st for every Cuff row; this will be the edge upon which the Hand is worked), ch 1, turn work 90 degrees clockwise, sl st in next 5 chs along beg-ch edge, ch 28, working through bottom bump of each ch, sl st in 2nd ch from hook and next 26 chs (Upper Left Wave made), sl st in next 7 chs along beg-ch edge, ch 28, working through bottom bump of each ch, sl st in 2nd ch from hook and next 26 chs (Lower Left Wave made), sl st in last ch, fasten off.

Hand

Note: The Hand is worked in joined rows.
Working along sl st row from last row worked and using larger hook, join A to 11th (14th) sl st from left edge.
Row 1 (RS): Working in blo of each sl st, ch 1, sc in same st, ch 1, sk next 2 sl sts, [sc in next sl st, ch 1, sk next 2 sl sts] 2 (3) times, sc in next sl st, ch 1, sk last sl st, bringing right edge of Cuff around, sk 1st sl st, [sc in next sl st, ch 1, sk next 2 sl sts] 11 (13) times, join with sl st to beg sc using B, turn—15 (18) sc, 15 (18) sl sts.
Row 2 (WS): With B, work Linen Stitch patt across, join with sl st to beg sc using A, turn.
Row 3: With A, work Linen Stitch patt across, join with sl st to beg sc using B, turn.
Row 4: Rep Row 2.

Thumb Gusset

Row 1 (RS): With A, [sc in next ch-1 sp, ch 1, sk next sc] 12 (14) times, [sc, ch 1, sc] in next ch-1 sp, ch 1, sk next sc, [sc in next ch-1 sp, ch 1, sk next sc] 2 (3) times, join with sl st to beg sc using B, turn—2 sts inc'd, 16 (19) sc, 16 (19) sl sts.
WS Rows 2, 4, 6, 8: With B, work Linen Stitch patt across, join with sl st to beg sc using A, turn.
Row 3: With A, [sc in next ch-1 sp, ch 1, sk next sc] 12 (14) times, sc in next ch-1 sp, ch 1, sc in next sc, ch 1, [sc in next ch-1 sp, ch 1, sk next sc] 3 (4) times, turn—17 (20) sc, 17 (20) sl sts.
Row 5: With A, [sc in next ch-1 sp, ch 1, sk next sc] 13 (15) times, [sc, ch 1, sc] in next ch-1 sp, ch 1, sk next sc, [sc in next ch-1 sp, ch 1, sk next sc] 3 (4) times, join with sl st to beg sc using B, turn—18 (21) sc, 18 (21) sl sts.
Row 7: With A, [sc in next ch-1 sp, ch 1, sk next sc] 13 (15) times, sc in next ch-1 sp, ch 1, sc in next sc, ch 1, [sc in next ch-1 sp, ch 1, sk next sc] 4 (5) times, turn—19 (22) sc, 19 (22) sl sts.

Row 9: With A, [sc in next ch-1 sp, ch 1, sk next sc] 14 (16) times, [sc, ch 1, sc] in next ch-1 sp, ch 1, sk next sc, [sc in next ch-1 sp, ch 1, sk next sc] 4 (5) times, join with sl st to beg sc using B, turn—20 (23) sc, 20 (23) sl sts.

Row 10: Rep Row 2.

Medium/Large Size Only

Row 11 (RS): With A, [sc in next ch-1 sp, ch 1, sk next sc] 16 times, sc in next ch-1 sp, ch 1, sc in next sc, ch 1, [sc in next ch-1 sp, ch 1, sk next sc] 6 times, join with sl st to beg sc using B, turn—24 sc, 24 sl sts.

Row 12: With B, work Linen Stitch patt across, join with sl st to beg sc using A, turn.

Upper Hand

Row 1 (RS): With A, [sc in next ch-1 sp, ch 1, sk next sc] 11 (13) times, sc in next ch-1 sp, ch 1, sk next 11 (13) sts, [sc in next ch-1 sp, ch 1, sk next sc] 3 (4) times, join with sl st to beg sc using B, turn—30 (36) sts.

Row 2 (WS): With B, work Linen Stitch patt across, join with sl st to beg sc using A, turn—15 (18) sc, 15 (18) sl sts.

Row 3: With A, work Linen Stitch patt across, join with sl st to beg sc using A, turn.

Rows 4–8 (4–10): Rep Rows 2–3, 2 (3) more times, then rep Row 2. Cut B.

Row 9 (11): With A, work Linen Stitch patt across, join with sl st to beg sc, do not turn.

Switch to smaller hook.

Row 10 (12): Ch 1, sc in same st, sc in each sc and sp around, join with sl st to beg sc.

Row 11 (13): Ch 1, bpsc around same st, bpsc around each st around, fasten off.

Thumb

With smaller hook, join A with sl st to center of Thumb gap.

Rnd 1: Ch 1, work 2 sc along gap, sc in next 11 (13) Thumb sts and sps, work 1 sc along rem side of gap, join with sl st to beg sc—14 (16) sc.

Rnd 2: Ch 1, bpsc around same st, bpsc around each st around, fasten off.

Left Mitt

Cuff

Work as for Right Mitt.

Hand

Note: The Hand is worked in joined rows.

Working along sl st row from last row worked and using larger hook, join A to 11th (14th) sl st from right edge.

Row 1 (RS): Working in blo of each sl st, ch 1, sc in same st, ch 1, sk next 2 sl sts, [sc in next sl st, ch 1, sk next 2 sl sts] 10 (12) times, sc in next sl st, ch 1, sk last sl st, bringing right edge of Cuff around, sk 1st sl st, [sc in next sl st, ch 1, sk next 2 sl sts] 3 (4) times, join with sl st to beg sc using B, turn—15 (18) sc, 15 (18) sl sts.

Row 2 (WS): With B, work Linen Stitch patt across, join with sl st to beg sc using A, turn.

Row 3: With A, work Linen Stitch patt across, join with sl st to beg sc using A, turn.

Row 4: Rep Row 2.

Thumb Gusset

Row 1 (RS): With A, [sc in next ch-1 sp, ch 1, sk next sc] 2 (3) times, [sc, ch 1, sc] in next ch-1 sp, ch 1, sk next sc, [sc in next ch-1 sp, ch 1, sk next sc] 12 (14) times, join with sl st to beg sc using B, turn—16 (19) sc, 16 (19) sl sts.

WS Rows 2, 4, 6, 8: With B, work Linen Stitch patt across, join with sl st to beg sc using A, turn.

Row 3: With A, [sc in next ch-1 sp, ch 1, sk next sc] 2 (3) times, sc in next ch-1 sp, ch 1, sc in next sc, ch 1, [sc in next ch-1 sp, ch 1, sk next sc] 13 (15) times, turn—17 (20) sc, 17 (20) sl sts.

Row 5: With A, [sc in next ch-1 sp, ch 1, sk next sc] 3 (4) times, [sc, ch 1, sc] in next ch-1 sp, ch 1, sk next sc, [sc in next ch-1 sp, ch 1, sk next sc] 13 (15) times, join with sl st to beg sc using B, turn—18 (21) sc, 18 (21), sl sts.

Row 7: With A, [sc in next ch-1 sp, ch 1, sk next sc] 3 (4) times, sc in next ch-1 sp, ch 1, sc in next sc, ch 1, [sc in next ch-1 sp, ch 1, sk next sc] 14 (16) times, turn—19 (22) sc, 19 (22) sl sts.

Row 9: With A, [sc in next ch-1 sp, ch 1, sk next sc] 4 (5) times, [sc, ch 1, sc] in next ch-1 sp, ch 1, sk next sc, [sc in next ch-1 sp, ch 1, sk next sc] 14 (16) times, join with sl st to beg sc using B, turn—20 (23) sc, 20 (23) sl sts.

Row 10: Rep Row 2.

Medium/Large Size Only

Row 11 (RS): With A, [sc in next ch-1 sp, ch 1, sk next sc] 5 times, sc in next ch-1 sp, ch 1, sc in next sc, ch 1, [sc in next ch-1 sp, ch 1, sk next sc] 17 times, join with sl st to beg sc using B, turn—24 sc, 24 sl sts.

Row 12: With B, work Linen Stitch patt across, join with sl st to beg sc using A, turn.

Upper Hand

Row 1 (RS): With A, [sc in next ch-1 sp, ch 1, sk next sc] 2 (3) times, sc in next ch-1 sp, ch 1, sk next 11 (13) sts, [sc in next ch-1 sp, ch 1, sk next sc] 12 (14) times, join with sl st to beg sc using B, turn—30 (36) sts.

Rows 2–11 (2–13): Work as for Right Mitt.

Thumb

Work as for Right Mitt.

Finishing

Cuff

With B, sl st along entire length of Upper and Lower Right Waves and Upper and Lower Left Waves. Weave in ends.

Lower Left Wave

Beg at tip of Lower Left Wave, roll into a coil so that the B sl sts are showing on the top. As you coil, secure on the underside with small tacking stitches using sewing needle and thread. When there is about 1"/2.5 cm remaining of the Lower Left Wave that is uncoiled, bring the Lower Right Wave up, around, and back over to its original position so that the ties are now "linked." Sew Lower Left Wave to Cuff leaving the overlapping 1"/2.5 cm unsewn, using photos on page 110 as a guide.

Lower Right Wave

Roll into a coil as for Lower Left Wave, tacking underside into place with small stitches and leaving the last 1"/2.5 cm unsewn. Sew to Cuff using photos as a guide.

Upper Left Wave

Roll into a coil, tacking underside into place with small stitches. When there are about 2"/5 cm remaining of the Upper Left Wave that are uncoiled, bring the Upper Right Wave up, around, and back over to its original position so that the ties are now "linked." Sew Upper Left Wave to Cuff, sew along the first 1"/2.5 cm that is uncoiled, leaving the remaining 1"/2.5 cm left unsewn.

Upper Right Wave

Roll into a coil as for Upper Left Wave, tacking underside into place with small stitches and leaving the last 1"/2.5 cm left unsewn. Sew to Cuff using photos as a guide.

How to Use This Book

The following are some basics you'll want to familiarize yourself with. These pertain not only to the mitts in this book, but will help you with other crochet projects as well.

Yarn

The specific yarn used is listed in the materials section for each project. If the yarn used is not available to you or you'd like to try something different, go for it! You'll want to take note of two important things: yarn weight and gauge.

The CYCA (Craft Yarn Council of America) classifies yarn weight as ranging from #0 lace weight to #6 super bulky (see chart on this page). The weights of yarn used in this book range from #0 lace weight to #4 medium. If you'd like to use a different yarn than is called for in the pattern, be sure to pick one that is the same weight as the yarn used.

STANDARDS & GUIDELINES FOR CROCHET AND KNITTING

Standard Yarn Weight System

Categories of yarn, gauge ranges, and recommended needle and hook sizes

Yarn Weight Symbol & Category Names	0 Lace	1 Super Fine	2 Fine	3 Light	4 Medium	5 Bulky	6 Super Bulky
Type of Yarns in Category	Fingering, 10 count crochet thread	Sock, Fingering, Baby	Sport, Baby	DK, Light Worsted	Worsted, Afghan, Aran	Chunky, Craft, Rug	Bulky, Roving
Knit Gauge Range* in Stockinette Stitch to 4 inches	33–40** sts	27–32 sts	23–26 sts	21–24 sts	16–20 sts	12–15 sts	6–11 sts
Recommended Needle in Metric Size Range	1.5–2.25 mm	2.25–3.25 mm	3.25–3.75 mm	3.75–4.5 mm	4.5–5.5 mm	5.5–8 mm	8 mm and larger
Recommended Needle U.S. Size Range	000 to 1	1 to 3	3 to 5	5 to 7	7 to 9	9 to 11	11 and larger
Crochet Gauge* Ranges in Single Crochet to 4 inches	32-42 double crochets**	21–32 sts	16–20 sts	12–17 sts	11–14 sts	8–11 sts	5–9 sts
Recommended Hook in Metric Size Range	Steel*** 1.6–1.4mm Regular hook 2.25 mm	2.25–3.5 mm	3.5–4.5 mm	4.5–5.5 mm	5.5–6.5 mm	6.5–9 mm	9 mm and larger
Recommended Hook U.S. Size Range	Steel*** 6, 7, 8 Regular hook B–1	B–1 to E–4	E–4 to 7	7 to I–9	I–9 to K–10½	K–10½ to M–13	M–13 and larger

* GUIDELINES ONLY: The above reflect the most commonly used gauges and needle or hook sizes for specific yarn categories.

** Lace weight yarns are usually knitted or crocheted on larger needles and hooks to create lacy, openwork patterns. Accordingly, a gauge range is difficult to determine. Always follow the gauge stated in your pattern.

*** Steel crochet hooks are sized differently from regular hooks—the higher the number, the smaller the hook, which is the reverse of regular hook sizing.

This Standards & Guidelines chart and downloadable symbol artwork are available at: **YarnStandards.com**

Gauge

Gauge, or tension, refers to how many stitches and rows/rounds in a particular stitch you should be crocheting per inch (for example, 20 sts x 20 rows in single crochet = 4"/10 cm square).

Typically, it is very important to do what is called a gauge swatch—a sample of the size called for in the gauge information, using the yarn and hook you plan to use for the project—to determine if you are getting the correct gauge. If your gauge is too loose (fewer stitches per inch than called for) or too tight (more stitches per inch), then you need to adjust your hook size. For loose gauge, go down in hook size. If your gauge is too tight, try using a larger hook. For this book, I say forget the gauge swatch (even though I do tell you what the gauge should be for each project)! The beauty of fingerless gloves and mittens is that the projects are all small to begin with, so they're really just big swatches. I recommend casting on for a project to start. If after a couple of inches you see that your gauge is off, start again with the appropriate hook size.

Sizing

Each pattern in this book indicates finished hand circumference and length. To determine the size you'd like to make, first ask yourself if the mitt will be for yourself or someone else. If it is for you, measure all the way around your hand just above your thumb. This is your actual hand circumference. In most cases, it is better for your mitt to have no ease or just a little bit of positive ease, meaning the finished mitt should be your actual hand measurement or a little bit more. Because crochet does not typically have very much elasticity, you need to make sure there is enough ease to get it on your hand. If you're making one of the projects to give as a gift, refer to the following standard measurements for hand circumference:

- Women (small): $6^1/_2$–7"
- Women (medium): $7^1/_2$–8"
- Women (large): $8^1/_2$–9"
- Men (small): $7^1/_2$–8"
- Men (medium): $8^1/_2$–9"
- Men (large): $9^1/_2$–$10^1/_2$"

Reading Charts

Because crochet stitches are not usually square, crochet charts are typically not made of right angles either! Many patterns in this book have at least one chart with the pattern, but there are also written instructions. Some people find it easiest to use either text or visual guides, which is why I have provided both. Even for those of you who find the written instruction easier to follow, referencing the chart can still be helpful at times when making sense of how things fit together.

Each chart contains numbers at the beginning of each row/round. These numbers visually have been placed at the start of the row or round. If the pattern is worked back and forth in rows, you will read right-side rows from right to left, and wrong side rows from left to right. Just start with the row number and work across. Each symbol in the chart is identified in the key. If there is an abbreviation you are unfamiliar with, be sure to check the abbreviations list.

Abbreviations

b	bobble
beg	beginning
blo	back loop only
bpdc	back post double crochet
bpdc2tog	back post double crochet 2 together—1 st dec'd
bphdc	back post half double crochet
bpsc	back post single crochet
bpsc2tog	back post single crochet 2 together—1 st dec'd
bpslst	back post slip stitch
bptr	back post triple crochet
CC	contrast color
ch(s)	chain(s)
cont	continued
dc	double crochet
dc2tog	double crochet 2 stitches together—1 st dec'd
dc-fpdc dec	double crochet front post double crochet decrease—1 st dec'd
dec'd	decreased
esc	extended single crochet
flo	front loop only
fpdc	front post double crochet
fpdc2tog	front post double crochet 2 together—1 st dec'd
fpdc sh	front post double crochet shell
fphdc	front post half double crochet
fpsc	front post single crochet
fpslst	front post slip stitch

fptr	front post triple crochet
fsc	foundation single crochet
hdc	half double crochet
inc'd	increased
LH	left hand
lp(s)	loop(s)
MC	main color
patt	pattern
rem	remain(ing)
rep	repeat
rev sc	reverse single crochet
rnd	round
RH	right hand
RS	right side
sc	single crochet
sc-b	single crochet with bead
sc2tog	single crochet 2 stitches together—1 st dec'd
sh	shell
sk	skip
sl st	slip stitch
sp(s)	space(s)
st(s)	stitch(es)
t-ch	turning chain
tr	triple crochet
WS	wrong side
yo	yarn over

Stitch and Technique Guide

This section covers most of the techniques used in this book, but not every single aspect of every pattern. Do not forget there is a wealth of information available on the Internet! A quick search of the web and sites like YouTube will result in many videos and tutorials on virtually any crochet technique you want to learn.

Anatomy of a Stitch

Here are the most commonly used basic stitches in crochet. From right to left are single crochet, half double crochet, double crochet, and triple crochet stitches. In each of these stitches, the front and back loops are the same. But the taller the stitch gets, the taller the post gets.

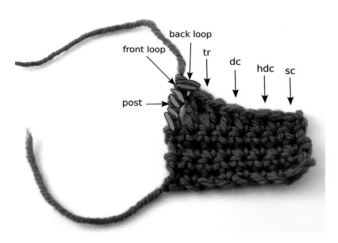

Getting Started

There are numerous ways to begin a project. The following techniques are the most common ways of doing so.

Slipknot

The very beginning of almost every crochet piece is a slipknot. It's the first step in the beginning chain. There are different methods of making a slipknot. Shown here is just one way of getting the job done.

1. Hold the yarn in both hands, leaving a tail several inches long.

2. Make a single loop with the yarn.

3. Rotate the loop so it's over the top of the strand that's coming from the ball of yarn.

(continued)

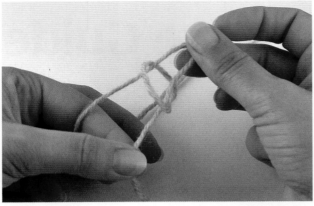

4. Pull the strand coming from the ball of yarn through the loop that was formed, making sure not to pull out the tail end from this loop.

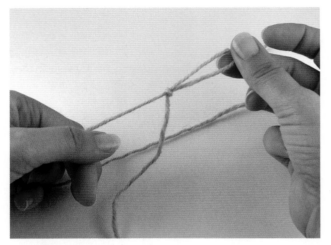

5. Tighten the knot securely.

6. Place your hook into the loop.

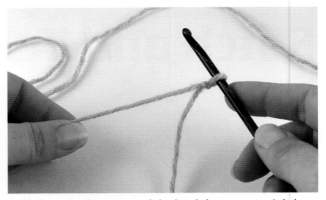

7. Tighten the loop around the hook, but not too tightly. The loop needs to be loose enough so that the hook moves back and forth easily.

Beginning Chain

Most crochet projects start with a beginning chain. This is a series of loops into which stitches will be worked. Try to work the beginning chain at an "average" tension. Working the chains too tightly makes it difficult to work the first row of stitches into them. Making the chains too loose can give a sloppy look to the edge. If you have difficulty making the chain loose and even, try going up one hook size for this beginning chain and returning to the hook size used for the remainder of the project after the chains are made.

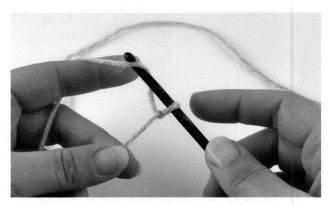

1. Make a slipknot and place it on your hook. Yarn over by bringing the yarn from back to front over the top of the hook.

2. Bring the yarn through the slipknot—1 chain formed.

3. Make as many chains as called for in the pattern. The loop on the hook does not count as a chain.

Working into the Chain

If you take a look at your crochet chain, you'll see that there are different parts of each chain. On the top of the chain, you can see that there is a V shape for each chain. These are called the top loops. The loop closest to you is the front top loop; the loop furthest from you is the back top loop. On the bottom side of the chain there are little bumps. These are called the bottom bumps. There are different reasons for working into different parts of the chain, depending on the final outcome of the beginning edge.

Here is what the top side of the chain looks like.

To work into the back top loop, insert your hook into the chain this way.

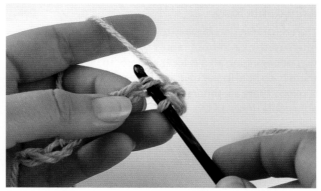

To work into both the back top loop and bottom bump, insert your hook into the chain this way. If a pattern does not specify, this is the most common way to begin.

Here is what the bottom side of the chain looks like.

(continued)

To work into the bottom bump, insert your hook into the chain this way.

Adjustable Ring

The adjustable ring is a way to begin work in the round. It is often used in center-out motifs and top-down hats. This way of beginning allows for the center to be tightened so there is no hole in the middle of the project. Like the slipknot, there are different methods of making an adjustable ring, and this is the way I do it.

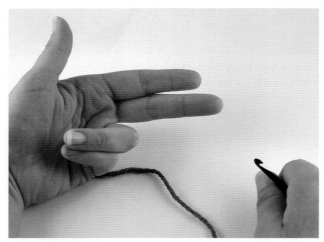

1. Hold out the index and middle fingers on your left hand.

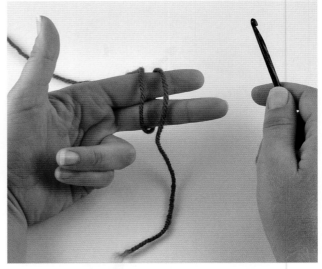

2. With the end in front, wrap the yarn clockwise around the two fingers $1^1/_2$ times so that the ball end of the yarn is hanging in the back.

3. Take the resulting ring off your fingers and hold the strands together, being careful that the ring does not come apart.

4. Insert the hook into the ring. Grab the back part of the loop which is attached to the ball end of the yarn, like a yarn over.

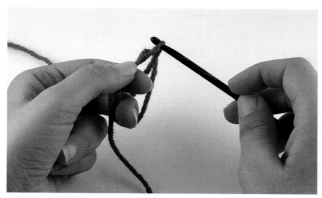

5. Pull this strand through the ring.

6. Yarn over.

7. Pull the yarn over through the ring.

8. Chain 1 made. You are now ready to begin working single crochets into the ring. If the beginning round in the ring was going to be half double crochet, you would chain 2; for double crochet, chain 3, and so on.

9. Insert your hook into the ring and yarn over.

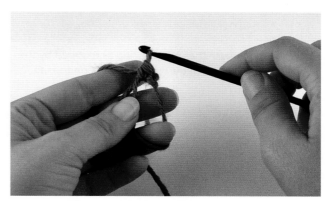

10. Complete the single crochet.

(continued)

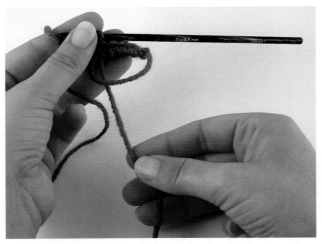

11. Work a few more stitches into the ring. Tighten up the ring some by pulling on the tail. It is easier to work into the ring when it is not too loose.

12. Work as many stitches into the ring as required by the pattern. Fully tighten the ring by pulling on the tail.

Working in the Round

To work a project in the round, you can begin by making a chain and then joining the chain to create a big ring. Many of the mitts in this book use this technique.

1. Make as many chains as specified in the pattern.

2. Bring the beginning of the chain around as shown, taking care to not twist it and keeping the top portion of the chain (the side with the Vs) to the outside.

3. To join, insert your hook into the top back loop and bottom bump.

4. Yarn over.

5. Complete the slip stitch by pulling the yarn over through.

6. To begin the first round of stitches, chain as many as specified for the pattern, usually 1 if the first round is single crochet.

7. Make the first stitch in the same space where the slip stitch was made.

First single crochet complete.

Basic Stitches

This is an overview of the most frequently used stitches in both crochet and the patterns in this book.

Single Crochet (sc)

Aside from the slip stitch, this is the shortest crochet stitch. A fabric made from single crochet is dense and has the tendency to curl. If single crochet is worked through only the back loop on every row, a sort of ribbing can be made.

1. Insert your hook through both top loops of the next stitch. Yarn over.

(continued)

2. Pull the yarn over through—2 loops on the hook. Yarn over.

2. Insert your hook into the next stitch.

3. Pull the yarn over through both loops on the hook—1 single crochet made.

3. Yarn over.

Double Crochet (dc)

This stitch is about two times as high as the single crochet. A fabric made from double crochets does not usually curl, and is more open than single crochet.

4. Pull the yarn over through—3 loops on the hook.

1. Before inserting your hook into the next stitch, yarn over.

5. Yarn over.

6. Pull the yarn over through the first 2 loops on the hook—2 loops remain on the hook.

7. Yarn over.

8. Pull the yarn over through the remaining 2 loops on the hook—1 double crochet made.

Half Double Crochet (hdc)

This stitch is about one and a half times as high as a single crochet. It's taller than a single crochet, but shorter than a double crochet. A fabric made from half double crochet is fairly dense and does not curl.

1. Before inserting your hook into the next stitch, yarn over.

2. Insert your hook into the next stitch. Yarn over.

(continued)

3. Pull the yarn over through the hook—3 loops on the hook.

2. Insert your hook into the next stitch. Yarn over.

4. Yarn over and pull through all 3 loops on the hook—1 half double crochet made.

3. Pull the yarn over through—4 loops on the hook.

Triple Crochet (tr)

This stitch is about three times as high as the single crochet. Triple crochets make for a very open fabric and work up quickly.

4. Yarn over and pull through 2 loops on the hook—3 loops remain on the hook.

1. Before inserting your hook into the next stitch, yarn over 2 times.

5. Yarn over and pull through 2 loops on the hook again—2 loops remain on the hook.

6. Yarn over and pull through the remaining 2 loops on the hook—1 triple crochet made.

Post Stitches

Post stitches, also sometimes called *relief* stitches, are worked around the post of stitches from a previous row. They are typically worked with double crochets. Post stitches can be worked from the front (front post stitches) or the back (back post stitches). They are used to create texture, cables, the look of ribbing, and more.

Front Post Double Crochet (fpdc)

1. Yarn over.

2. From right to left, insert your hook through the post of the stitch indicated from the front of the work, usually the stitch below the next stitch on your work.

3. Yarn over.

4. Pull the yarn over through—3 loops on the hook.

(continued)

5. Yarn over and pull through 2 loops on the hook—2 loops remain on the hook.

6. Yarn over and pull through the remaining 2 loops on the hook—1 front post double crochet made.

Several front post double crochets made.

Back Post Double Crochet (bpdc)

1. Yarn over.

2. From right to left, insert your hook through the post of the stitch indicated from the back of the work. View from the front side shown.

View from the back side shown.

3. Yarn over.

5. Complete as for a front post double crochet by working a yarn over and pulling through 2 loops on the hook, 2 times—1 back post double crochet made.

4. Pull the yarn over through—3 loops on the hook.

Several back post double crochets made.

View from the back side shown.

View from the back side shown.

Decreases

Decreases are just that—reducing the number of stitches you have. There are different methods of decreasing stitches. The following two examples show how to work two stitches together to make one stitch.

Single Crochet Two Stitches Together (sc2tog)

1. Insert your hook into the next stitch. Yarn over.

2. Pull the yarn over through the stitch—2 loops on the hook.

3. Insert your hook into the next stitch. Yarn over.

4. Pull the yarn over through the stitch—3 loops on the hook.

5. Yarn over.

6. Pull the yarn over through all 3 loops on the hook—1 stitch decreased.

Double Crochet Two Stitches Together (dc2tog)

1. Yarn over.

2. Insert your hook into the next stitch. Yarn over.

3. Pull the yarn over through the stitch—3 loops on the hook.

4. Yarn over and pull through the first 2 loops—2 loops remain on the hook.

5. Yarn over.

6. Insert your hook into the next stitch. Yarn over.

(continued)

7. Pull the yarn over through the stitch—4 loops on the hook.

8. Yarn over and pull through the first 2 loops—3 loops on the hook.

9. Yarn over and pull through the first 2 loops on the hook, 2 times—1 stitch decreased.

Changing Colors

Tapestry and Fair Isle are the two primary methods of changing colors in crochet. They have their differences but also things in common. In tapestry crochet, stitches are worked around with all the colors being carried along. In Fair Isle, the unused color(s) are held to the back until needed, forming what are called floats between stitches of the same color. In both types of colorwork, there is one key technique in common. When changing colors, the first half of the stitch is worked in one color but finished with the color that is going to be used in the following stitch.

Tapestry Crochet

This is typically worked in single crochet. In this type of colorwork, each color that is being used in the round is carried along throughout the entire round. Whichever color is being used for a particular stitch is worked around the strands of the other colors that are being carried. When it is time to use a new color, the old color is dropped, the new color is picked up, and this new color is worked around the other strands as well. The tapestry/Fair Isle crochet pattern in this book instructs you to work stitches through the back loop only. Tapestry can be worked through both loops, but I prefer the look of the stitches when worked through only the back loop. They line up better vertically and avoid most of the right-slanting behavior normally seen. Prudent times to use tapestry crochet are in a pattern that has just a few contrast color stitches, when more than two colors are used, and/or when the space between color changes is long.

Single Crochet with No Color Change

1. The working yarn or color is held and tensioned as usual while the other color(s) is held down next to the current row of stitches.

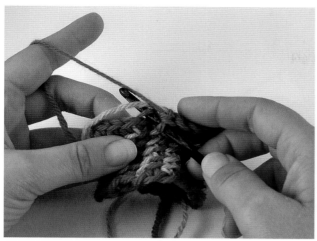

2. Insert your hook into the back loop of the next stitch, underneath the other strand(s).

3. Yarn over and pull through the stitch—2 loops on the hook.

4. Complete the single crochet by yarning over and pulling through the 2 loops.

Single Crochet with Color Change

1. If the *next* stitch will be worked in a new color, begin the single crochet in the same way, by yarning over and pulling through the stitch—first half of the single crochet complete.

2. Drop the color you were working with and pick up the new color.

3. Yarn over with the new color and pull through the 2 loops on the hook—single crochet and color change complete.

Fair Isle

As with tapestry crochet, Fair Isle is usually done using single crochet stitches. And like tapestry, I prefer the look of Fair Isle worked through the back loop only, rather than both loops. It is easiest to work Fair Isle using just two colors at a time in a given round. The following photos show the technique worked by holding one color in each hand. To maintain even tension, keep the same color in each hand throughout the piece. This method can take some practice. If you prefer, you might try dropping the color not in use instead.

1. In the piece shown, blue and tan stitches have been alternated every other stitch. A blue stitch was just worked.

2. To work the next (tan) stitch, insert your hook into the next stitch, keeping the blue strand to the back and out of the way.

3. Yarn over with tan by bringing the yarn around the hook as shown.

4. Pull the yarn over through the stitch—2 loops on the hook. The blue strand is still in back and out of the way.

5. Because the next stitch will be a blue stitch, yarn over with blue, keeping the tan strand in back and out of the way.

6. Pull the yarn over through both loops on the hook—1 single crochet made.

Special Techniques

Short Rows

Just as the name implies, short rows are rows that are not complete, full rows. They are used to create wedge shaping for both decorative and functional purposes.

1. Work to the stitch indicated in your pattern.

2. Turn your work, chain 1.

3. Place a safety pin or removable marker in the chain 1.

4. Work back to the beginning of the row as indicated in your pattern, and then back again to the turning point.

(continued)

5. Insert your hook through the marked turning chain—2 loops on the hook. Remove the safety pin or marker.

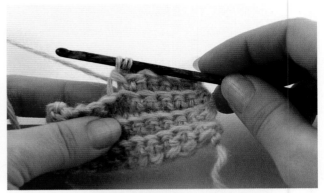

8. Pull the yarn over through 2 loops on the hook—2 loops remain on the hook.

6. Insert your hook through the next stitch—3 loops on the hook.

9. Yarn over and pull through both loops on the hook—joining single crochet completed.

7. Yarn over.

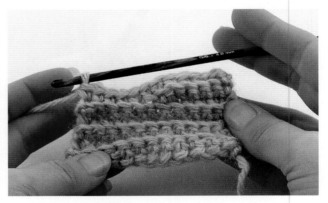

10. Continue as indicated in your pattern.

Hairpin Lace

Worked on a special loom, this is a different sort of way to make lace. Most hairpin lace looms have adjustable widths, so that the strip of lace being made is customizable. Castlerock Mitts (page 62) incorporate a single strip of hairpin lace on the top of the hand. But this technique can be used in many other applications.

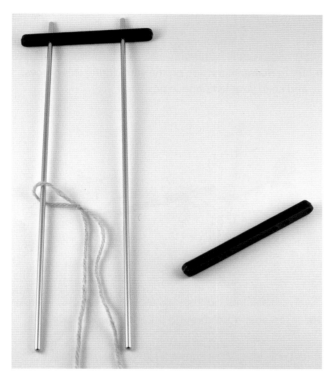

1. Take off the bottom part of the loom. Make a slipknot and place it on the left prong of the loom. The knot in the slipknot should be approximately centered between the two prongs. Replace the bottom of the loom.

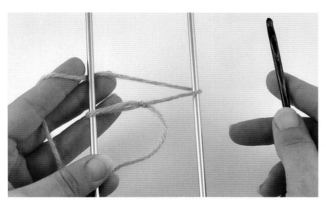

2. Take the yarn across the front of the loom and around the back over the right prong.

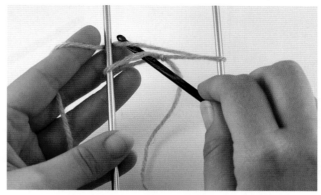

3. Insert your hook through the slipknot and yarn over.

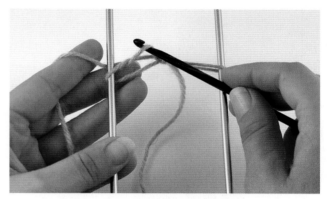

4. Pull the yarn over through the slipknot.

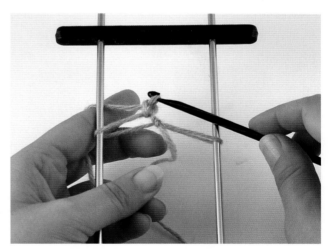

5. Chain 1.

(continued)

6. Remove your hook from the chain, being careful not to undo your work.

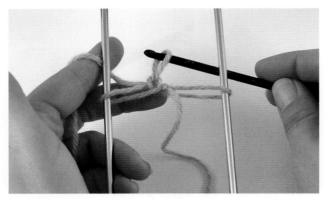

7. Reinsert your hook through the chain from the back of the loom.

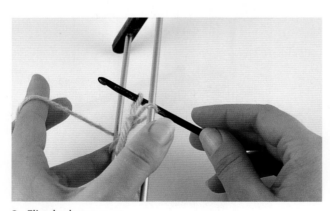

8. Flip the loom over.

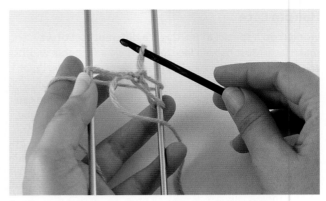

9. Try to maintain tension on the yarn during this process and keep your left hand in position.

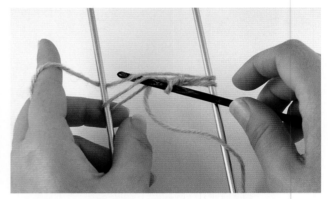

10. Insert your hook through the left loop. Yarn over.

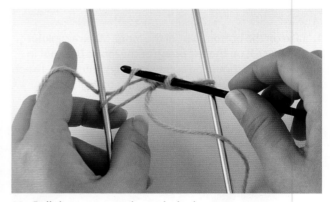

11. Pull the yarn over through the loop.

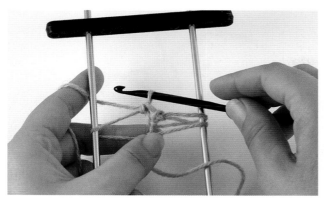

12. Chain 1 to complete the stitch.

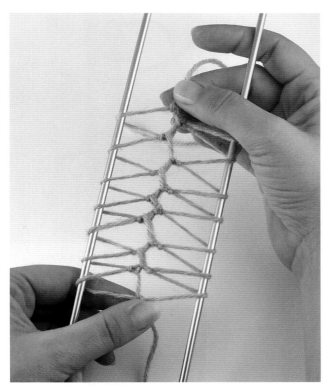

13. Repeat steps 6–12 until your hairpin lace strip has as many loops on each side as the pattern calls for. Finish by fastening off the last chain 1, leaving a tail several inches long.

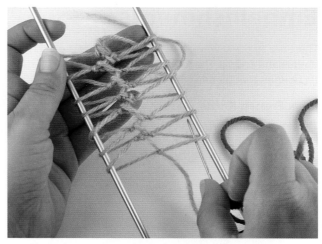

14. Thread waste yarn through a tapestry needle. Pass the needle through the live loops on the right prong, taking care to enter each loop in the same direction.

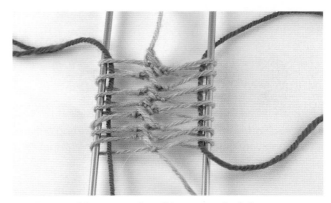

15. Repeat this process for all loops on the left prong.

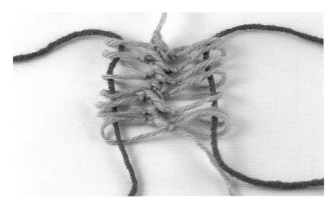

16. Remove the strip from the loom. Keep the waste yarn in the loops during the joining process of the strip. Remove the waste yarn only once all the loops have been joined.

Embellishments

There are so many ways to make your crochet projects unique and special. The following are just a couple of techniques that pertain to specific projects in this book.

Faux French Knots

These little knots form the eyes on the icons for the Emotimitts on page 102. True French knots are difficult to execute in worsted weight yarn, so this is a good substitute.

3. First knot complete.

1. Thread your yarn through a tapestry needle and pull through your crochet piece. Leave a tail several inches long.

4. Make another overhand knot around the first knot.

2. Make an overhand knot.

5. Second knot complete.

6. Insert your tapestry needle back through the piece just to the side of where it came out originally.

7. Faux French knot complete. After all the knots are completed, secure the yarn at the back of the work.

Applied Crochet Lines

These lines, along with applied circles, are used in Raindrops on page 58. This technique is simply working slip stitches on an existing piece of crochet.

This is a piece of crochet worked entirely in slip stitch crochet, just as the base mitt in Raindrops is worked.

1. Hold the yarn for the lines beneath the work. Insert your hook from the front to the back through the center of the stitch indicated.

2. Yarn over beneath the piece.

(continued)

3. Pull the yarn over through to the front of the work.

4. Moving up the piece, insert your hook from the front to the back of the center of the next stitch.

5. Yarn over beneath the piece.

6. Pull the yarn over through to the front of the work—2 loops on the hook.

7. Pull the yarn over through the first loop on the hook—1 slip stitch made.

8. Repeat steps 4–8 for as many chains as are required.

Applied Circles

These circles are used at the end of applied lines, also in the Raindrops project. This takes the technique of applied lines one step further to create a shape. Try using these ideas to come up with your own way of decorating your mitts!

1. To the right of the applied line just worked, skip over two rows of slip stitch crochet (visually this will be one row of Vs and one stitch up. Insert your hook into this stitch.

2. Chain 1 by working steps 5–8 of Applied Lines. Insert your hook through the next stitch up in the same row of stitches.

3. Chain 1. To the left of the 2 chains just made, skip over two rows of crochet and one stitch up. Insert your hook into this stitch.

4. Chain 1. This chain forms the top of the circle.

5. To the left of the chain just made, skip over two rows of crochet and one stitch down. Insert your hook into this stitch.

(continued)

6. Chain 1.

7. Insert your hook into the next stitch down.

8. Chain 1. It will be easier to turn your work 180 degrees at this point.

9. Insert your hook through the center of the last stitch from your Applied Line, the last chain made before the first chain of your Applied Circle.

10. Pull the yarn tail through. Trim the tail so it is several inches long.

11. Thread the tail through a tapestry needle. Insert the needle through the center of the same stitch.

12. Pull the tail through to the back of the work and secure.

Finishing

Finishing your project properly is just as important as the making.

Mattress Stitch

There are numerous ways to join pieces of fabric together, but this is my go-to method. Mattress stitch produces a seam that is invisible and sturdy. When pulling the yarn taut in the seam, be sure not to pull too tightly or the fabric will pucker. Shown here, this seam is worked on the ends of pieces of crochet. It can also be used to join pieces side to side, or end to side.

1. Lay out your pieces with the ends to be joined together, with the right sides of the pieces facing up. Thread the seaming yarn through a tapestry needle. Insert the tapestry needle underneath both top loops of the first stitch on the right piece.

2. Insert the needle underneath both top loops of the first stitch on the left piece.

3. Pull the yarn through.

4. Insert the needle back into the right piece in the same spot where the yarn exited before.

(continued)

5. Bring the needle out 1 stitch over.

6. Insert the needle into the left piece in the same spot where the yarn exited before.

7. Bring the needle out 1 stitch over.

8. Repeat steps 4–7 a few more times.

9. Pull the yarn taut.

10. Continue pulling the yarn until the seam is invisible. Take care not to pull so tightly that the pieces being joined gather and pucker. Repeat steps 4–7 along the entire length of the seam, pulling the seaming yarn taut every couple of inches.

Blocking

Blocking is not just for sports! It's often a very important step in finishing your crocheted piece. Blocking refers to the process of smoothing and/or stretching your fabric. It can take your finished piece from *eh. . .* to *Wow!* There are many factors that can affect whether or not to block, and what type of blocking method to use. The two methods I rely on are wet blocking and steam blocking.

Wet Blocking

Wet blocking is the method I use most frequently and it is safe on any fiber. Depending on the fiber, you will want to use either cold or warm water. Be sure to check your yarn label to see what it recommends. To wet block a glove or mitten, submerge it in water with a bit of wool wash. It's a good idea to use wool wash even on nonwool fibers because it is less harsh than detergent. Let the glove soak for a few minutes; don't leave it to soak for long. Rinse it out thoroughly. Some yarns will bleed color. Be sure to continue rinsing until the water runs clear. Gently fold the glove and press out excess water; don't wring your glove! Then roll it in a towel, soaking up as much moisture as you can. Lay your glove on a blocking mat or other surface that won't incur water damage. Carefully pat and lightly stretch the glove into shape, smoothing out any unevenness in stitches. For colorwork gloves, blocking is especially important in evening out stitches. You may have to be a little more forceful when blocking these. Once your glove is in shape and smooth, let it dry. That's it!

Steam Blocking

There are special garment steamers available for steam blocking, but it's often hard to control temperature on these. An iron is nice because you can control the amount of steam and the temperature. It's typically not a good idea to go too steam-crazy on crocheted items, as it can give the crocheted fabric a "wilted" effect and make it limp and lifeless. Again, be sure to check your yarn label to see what it recommends. But honestly, even for a yarn that does not recommend ironing, a light steaming is probably not going to harm it.

To steam block, lay out your glove. With the iron set on a low to medium setting, hold it at least 2 inches above the glove. Pass the iron slowly back and forth over the top of the piece. You will see the stitches react to the steam, sort of settling into place. After steaming, let the piece dry.

I will sometimes try steam blocking before wet blocking as it is not as time consuming and doesn't take as long to dry.

There are some projects in this book that do not mention blocking in the finishing instructions. This is because with the combination of stitch patterns and yarn used, I personally did not find it necessary to do so. This may not be true for you! If your glove turns out a little uneven here and there, even if the instructions don't specify to block, by all means *do!*

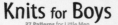
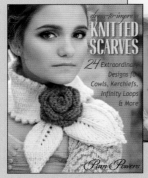

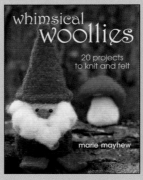

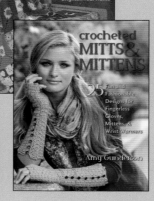